THE PATH OF
CENTERING
PRAYER

This work was supported by the Fetzer Institute

"This book in my view is the best, most comprehensive, and most practical book on centering prayer."

FATHER THOMAS KEATING Founder of
Contemplative Outreach and author of *Open Mind, Open Heart*

"In this beautiful book, David Frenette significantly expands the map of the known centering prayer universe. With the blessing of his spiritual father, Thomas Keating, David develops—and sometimes gently reshapes—fundamental building blocks of the centering prayer teaching. This is an important moment in the centering prayer lineage transmission, when a faithful student emerges into mastery, and David rises to the occasion with humility, gentleness, and radiance. His work will breathe significant new life into your personal practice. I have found my own practice much illumined by this book."

CYNTHIA BOURGEAULT
Author of *Centering Prayer and Inner Awakening*

"This excellent book represents Christianity come to maturity! Here you will find good theology, good practice, good psychology, and a recovery of the foundation itself—how to live in communion all the time."

FATHER RICHARD ROHR, OFM Founding Director
of the Center for Action and Contemplation

"This book has three qualities that make it so helpful to read. First, David Frenette is clearly speaking out of his experience of centering prayer as a path to God. This experiential voice cuts through theoretical explanations and helps us come to our own intimate desire to experience God's presence in our lives. Second, his frequent references to *The Cloud of Unknowing* and other classical texts of mystic teachers bear witness to this book's fidelity to the ancient and timeless wisdom of contemplative Christianity. And third, David guides us along the contemplative path in an inviting and accessible style—well suited to both sincere beginners and to those who are more well-seasoned in following the interior path that David Frenette invites us to follow."

JAMES FINLEY, PHD Core Teacher of the
Center for Action and Contemplation

"With simplicity and great wisdom, David Frenette reconnects you to the universal tradition of how to open to God, how to pray in silence, and finally, how to let the spirit pray within your heart. If you want, or need, to be drawn deeper into prayer, read this book and live its guidance."

LLEWELLYN VAUGHAN-LEE, PHD Sufi teacher and author of
Prayer of the Heart in Christian and Sufi Mysticism

"In his lucid guide to centering prayer, David Frenette navigates a path for beginners and seasoned practitioners who wish to enter ever-deepening states of loving friendship with the divine."

MIRABAI STARR Author of *God of Love: A Guide
to the Heart of Judaism, Christianity, and Islam*

"This wonderful book provides direction, encouragement, and support for a prayer practice with ancient roots. Drawing on his considerable experience as a spiritual director, David Frenette skillfully shares stories and offers wisdom that illuminates the heart of the practice and will lead practitioners through the subtle challenges that inevitably arise in the process of living into ever-deepening levels of prayer. This is a book not only to be read, but to be consulted regularly for insight and help along the way."

THE RIGHT REVEREND ROBERT O'NEILL
Bishop of the Episcopal Diocese of Colorado

"This book is a must-read for centering prayer practitioners! David enlightens readers with encouragement and enrichment, which will nourish them in their own commitment to the centering prayer practice and the contemplative life. It is the kind of book you pick up again and again."

GAIL FITZPATRICK-HOPLER
President of Contemplative Outreach

THE PATH OF CENTERING PRAYER

DEEPENING YOUR EXPERIENCE OF GOD

DAVID FRENETTE

with a foreword by
Father Thomas Keating

SOUNDS TRUE
Boulder, Colorado

Sounds True, Inc.
Boulder, CO 80306

Published 2012, 2017

Cover design by Sarah Chesnutt. Cover photo © Jeff Saward
Book design by Lisa Kerans

Printed in Canada

The basic guidelines of centering prayer (see the appendix) are © 2006 Contemplative Outreach, Ltd. and reprinted with its permission.

ISBN 978-1-62203-866-4 (paperback)

Library of Congress Cataloging-in-Publication Data

Frenette, David.
The path of centering prayer : deepening your experience of God /
David Frenette.
    p. cm.
Includes bibliographical references
ISBN 978-1-60407-673-8
1. Contemplation. I. Title.
BV5091.C7F74 2012
248.3--dc23

                    2012002814

Ebook ISBN 978-1-60407-893-0

10 9 8 7 6 5 4 3 2

*To Father Thomas Keating
and his centering prayer students*

CONTENTS

PART I

Deepening Your Centering Prayer Practice
in the Light of Contemplation

PART II

Contemplative Attitudes

ACKNOWLEDGMENTS

Writing a book on contemplative practice is a solitary activity, done in relationship with God. But because the revelation of contemplative practice happens when the divine life manifests in a community of seekers, in concrete circumstances, it is also true that a book on contemplative practice does not happen alone.

My immense gratitude goes to Father Thomas Keating for his commitment to God, his witness to selfless service, and for his belief in my work. I also want to thank his monastic community, St. Benedict's Monastery in Snowmass, Colorado, and their abbot, Father Joseph Boyle, for their support over the years.

I offer thanks to my colleagues who staffed the intensive retreats at the Garrison Institute, at which these teachings were brought together in their current form: Steve Standiford, Marie Howard, Mary Dwyer, and Maru Ladrón de Guevara. Steve gave generously in many ways, as a spiritual brother, including recording the teachings. Marie used her organizational gifts and created a place for the retreat in Contemplative Outreach. My special thanks go to Lindsay Boyer, who, after recently staffing these retreats, took time from her own writing to read and edit the manuscript based upon her own practice. Lindsay and her husband, Mark, were my gracious hosts in the Catskill Mountains for two weeks as she and I worked on the manuscript. My thanks also to Julie Saad, Cathy McCarthy, and Gail Fitzpatrick Hopler, who supported the development of the material in earlier forms.

Many others supported this book along the way. To mention a few: Sister Bernadette Teasdale; Terri Murphy and the community at the Denver Center for Contemplative Living; Pat Johnson, Mary Ann Matheson, and Sherry Dutelle at the Snowmass retreat center; John Congdon, Carol DiMarcello, Margaret Johnson, Grace Huffman, Joanne Warner, Bill Wagner and Contemplative Outreach of Colorado; Gail Fitzpatrick Hopler, Father Carl Arico, and Olsiana Habazaj at the Contemplative Outreach International Resource Center; Rev. Cynthia Bourgeault, who has been a source of support and encouragement; Catherine Le Dret and Jasmin Cori, who edited early chapters; my oldest spiritual friends, Sarah Harding, Bob Bartel, and Morgen Alwell; my newest spiritual friends, Peter Williams and Jeffrey Fuller; and my inquisitive and heartfelt students at Naropa University.

Special thanks to Eric Nelson, Wayne Ramsey, and David Addiss at the Fetzer Institute, who graciously stewarded this project through many phases.

I'd like to thank Tami Simon and all the amazing folks at Sounds True for their belief in the book and skilled commitment to quality, including Jennifer Brown, Matt Licata, Rebecca Tate, Amy Rost, Haven Iverson, Sarah Gorecki, and Jennifer Holder.

And finally, huge thanks to my wife, Donna Zerner, who brought her profound insights and wisdom to help shape the book at key moments. The Spirit animates and inspires my life through her radiant presence. I live in daily gratitude for her.

AUTHOR'S NOTE

When I cite texts from the Bible, I have used The New Oxford Annotated Bible, 2007. However, because there is not yet one Bible translation attuned to both gender-neutral language toward God and a contemplative understanding of scripture, a few biblical passages are taken from other translations, as noted.

God is a mystery beyond names, symbols, and forms, yet the Christian tradition uses names, symbols, and forms, often gendered, to refer to God. The Christian contemplative tradition, like other traditions, is being renewed for current times in inclusive language. As scholars attend to this important endeavor, I have chosen in this book to primarily use gender-neutral language when speaking of God, while generally retaining other authors' use of masculine pronouns in citations and the language of standard Bible translations.

Foreword

This, David Frenette's first book, speaks to the ongoing development of centering prayer, and his teaching is a superb contribution to it. David has the special gift for contemplative teaching, the ability to share centering prayer and its conceptual background as well as its place in the Christian tradition. He is a careful student of the Christian mystical life, having pursued it through years of prayer and solitude and, even more importantly, by having his prayer life purified, enriched, and expressed in community and in the service of others.

I am grateful for David's deep understanding of the contemplative life and the wisdom he is able to share from his own lived experience. He has developed the teaching of centering prayer beyond the fundamentals, while at the same time fully supporting the programs that are basic to the centering prayer ministry. David continues to explore how centering prayer, in its fullest expression, can reveal and transmit the incredible depth of the Christian faith. His teaching, based on actual experience, reveals the intimacy that God has made available to every human being and how unique God's love is for each person.

Since 1983, David has worked full time on the development of centering prayer practices, the support of its practitioners, and the growth of Contemplative Outreach, the international network of centering prayer communities. He attended my first intensive two-week centering prayer retreat in 1983, where the seeds of centering prayer ripened within the group and Contemplative Outreach was born. David went on to cofound a residential retreat community, which we called Chrysalis House. There he lived a temporary form of monastic lifestyle and trained others in intensive prayer, community life, and service. He worked with the other community members to develop the contemplative practices that later became the foundation of Contemplative Outreach's spirituality. When his ten-year commitment to this community ended, David fulfilled its vision by seeking to integrate his contemplative training into ordinary life. He worked with adolescents in a treatment center for addiction, pursued graduate studies in counseling psychology, and served as a contemplative spiritual director while continuing his own intensive retreat practice in order to research and develop resources, programs, and practices for advanced centering prayer students.

In this book, David describes four ways of practicing centering prayer, building upon the basic guidelines offered in centering prayer workshops. These four deepening ways of practicing centering prayer are based on the three sacred symbols—the sacred word, the sacred breath, and the sacred glance—plus a recently developed approach that might be called the sacred nothingness, which is pure contemplation. This last way is perhaps the most direct route to what Jesus called "prayer in secret" (Matthew 6:6), and David describes it with much helpful detail. He also presents interior attitudes that help centering prayer move into contemplation, making it easier for practitioners to deepen their experience of God.

This book is an example of how God continues to enlighten practitioners of centering prayer, opening up new depths of meaning and new aspects of the practice that encourage longtime practitioners to penetrate the mystery of God's infinite love and ultimately to be transformed into it. Although he is an accomplished teacher, advisor, and spiritual director, this book shows that David's primary spiritual gift is in bringing forth new dimensions and nuances of contemplative practice that are solidly rooted in the revelation of Christ that all Christian practices point to and flow from. This is an extremely important endeavor, for a spiritual tradition stagnates unless it continues to breathe new life into itself with practices and resources appropriate for longtime practitioners, new generations of seekers, and changing social conditions. David's long years of retreat and early experience at Chrysalis House trained him for this work, which might be called "contemplative research and development."

This book in my view is the best, most comprehensive and most practical book on centering prayer. In the course of this outstanding work, David offers many precious insights from his own centering prayer practice and from his years of companioning others on the Christian contemplative path. His lived experience of being a contemplative in ordinary daily life will be invaluable to those who aspire to do the same thing. He is an excellent advisor in practical affairs upon whose judgment I am happy to rely. He is one of God's greatest gifts to the work of centering prayer and to me.

—Thomas Keating

INTRODUCTION

This book is a handbook to Christian contemplation and the practice of centering prayer. A contemplative practice like centering prayer opens you to *experiencing God*. Learning the increasingly subtle ways of practicing centering prayer described in this book *deepens your experience of God*. This book shows you how to journey on the path of centering prayer, a path leading to interior union with Christ and increasing unity with all of life as it is found emerging in God. Although designed to show advanced practitioners how to deepen their centering prayer practice, *The Path of Centering Prayer* can also be used by beginners looking to establish such a practice.

Christian Contemplative Practice and Centering Prayer

Similar in many ways to meditation in other spiritual traditions, centering prayer is a method of silent, wordless prayer that comes out of the Christian contemplative tradition. Different contemplative practices have always existed in Christianity. Practices like the Jesus Prayer in the Orthodox Christian tradition, *lectio divina*—the "divine reading" of scripture—in the Roman Catholic tradition, and the silent worship of some Quaker and Protestant churches have provided means for experiencing the contemplative dimension of the Gospel. The practice of centering prayer is primarily based on the teaching of a classic spiritual text from the fourteenth century, *The Cloud of Unknowing*. These and every specific form of Christian contemplative practice are rooted in the teachings of

Jesus and in his resurrected presence as the Christ. While rooted in Christ's eternal presence and Jesus's historical teachings, each of these forms of Christian contemplative practice, like centering prayer, arose and were developed within the unique cultural conditions of the time.

Although it was preserved mainly in monasteries in recent centuries, in the last two generations, at the same time that Eastern forms of meditation became increasingly popular in the West, the Christian contemplative tradition has undergone a renewal. Christian contemplation was brought to public attention in the 1950s and 1960s through the work of such writers as the Trappist monk Thomas Merton. Merton's prolific and best-selling writings inspired millions and deepened the public's thirst for mystical knowledge.

In the 1970s, three other Trappists, William Meninger, Basil Pennington, and Thomas Keating, looked to ancient Christian sources to develop a simple method of silent prayer, centering prayer, that would meet this thirst for contemplative practice, especially for those living outside the monastery. Thomas Keating translated Christian mystical theology into modern, psychological terms and created an extensive support network, called Contemplative Outreach, to support the practice of centering prayer in ordinary life.

Centering prayer is now practiced by hundreds of thousands of people and is constantly being adopted by new seekers excited to discover a well-developed meditation method rooted in the Christian tradition. Contemporary people discover in centering prayer a way to understand, experientially, the meaning of Jesus's teachings and cultivate a relationship with the living God. Centering prayer is practiced by Christians of many different denominations and by many who are not aligned with any church, but who find that it helps them deepen their relationship with Christ. It is also practiced by many in twelve-step recovery programs as a means of developing a relationship with their own "higher power." And centering prayer has helped many prisoners find inner peace amidst the chaos and despair of jail.

Recent scientific research is beginning to show the physical, psychological, and communal benefits of practicing centering prayer. Its primary effect is in transforming the structures of inner consciousness, which gradually brings freedom from the separate-self sense and allows practitioners to experience greater compassion for other people.[1] Practicing centering prayer awakens one to deeper meaning, as life itself becomes a spiritual journey. With centering prayer and Christian contemplation, God becomes a living reality instead of just a fundamentalist belief.

My Own Introduction to Centering Prayer

I was first touched by God's transcendent mystery as a young child. In my dreams, I sensed that my life held a meaning deeper than any meaning society could provide and that my life path would include continual searching, self-sacrifice, and dedication to others. Christ was too close to be recognized during these childhood dreams, but after waking, I felt a deep, radiant, unifying stillness in the night's silence. I never even considered telling anyone about the dreams or the experiences; they were a private world, ineffable and set apart from the rest of my life.

Because I lacked any religious training, those early experiences lay dormant, unaffirmed by the world. I didn't have the religious language to even know to call this reality *God,* much less any training in meditation to bring it to life. Without any way to integrate these unnamed experiences into my consciousness, they soon receded from my conscious awareness.

But when I was nineteen, the early experiences reappeared in my consciousness and triggered an intense search for meaning. I learned how people over the centuries experienced, named, and described how to receive and respond to the transcendent. My adult life became a path of responding to the loving mystery that I learned to name *God*, an inner education in the practice of contemplation. After following Eastern forms of meditation for a few years, I said yes to the way this mystery was revealing itself to me and became a Christian when I was twenty-three. I first learned centering prayer from reading a book about it; I practiced centering prayer daily for three years and then began to go deeper with its practice through years of retreat, beginning with a two-week intensive retreat with Thomas Keating. This simple contemplative practice; my friendship with him, my spiritual father; and my involvement with contemplative community and service have helped shape my relationship with God for the last thirty years.

This book on the subtleties of contemplation and centering prayer reflects what I have searched for in my own life: the knowledge of how to better discipline yourself, what to do in practice as the contemplative journey deepens, and how to say yes to the transcendent mystery of life, God. The teachings in this book were developed over many years through my work as a spiritual director and retreat guide.

What You Will Find in This Book

Centering prayer involves consenting to God's presence and action within—beyond thoughts, images, and perceptions—in order to form a contemplative relationship with God. Centering prayer and contemplation are often seen as two ends of a continuum. Centering prayer is at the active end of the continuum, where your actions predominate. Contemplation is at the receptive end of the continuum, where God's actions predominate. While centering prayer involves symbols, contemplation leads beyond these surface forms into a living encounter with God, beyond concepts and symbols.

This book looks at ways to deepen your centering prayer practice in order to help orient you to receive the gift of contemplation. It illustrates how, over time, your own actions in centering prayer move you to become more receptive to contemplation—God's presence acting within you. With time and greater understanding, you experience how what you do in centering prayer and what God does in contemplation are not so separate.

In beginning centering prayer, you use a sacred symbol as a way of consenting to the presence and action of God. In the tradition of the spiritual classic *The Cloud of Unknowing,* you choose a one- or two-syllable word, such as *God, Jesus, amen, love, peace, stillness, faith,* or *trust,* to be that symbol. As Thomas Keating has written in *Open Mind, Open Heart,* and in the foreword to this book, you can also use your breath or a simple inward glance as your symbol, or even practice without a symbol, in the sacred nothingness of God. Whatever you choose, you practice with the intention of consenting to God. Part I of this book explores how to use each sacred symbol and how each way of deepening centering prayer may offer particular benefits in different seasons of your spiritual journey.

More important than the type of symbol you use, its content, or its meaning is the way you practice with this symbol, the attitude you bring to the prayer. Each chapter in Part II presents two contemplative attitudes that help you deepen your meditation practice. Practicing contemplation involves dispositions more than techniques, gestures more than concrete steps, perspectives more than black-and-white directions. Taken from oral teachings given on retreats and in classes, the stories, images, citations, and instructions are meant to evoke your own contemplative experience of God and invite you further along the path of transformation in Christ. Practicing the contemplative attitudes of Part II allows God—the reality in whom prayer and life is found—to become the source of what you do in centering prayer. These attitudes can also be used to enter more deeply into other forms of meditation.

The instructional chapters of Part I are meant to be read *along with* the chapters in Part II on the contemplative attitudes. In this way, images and stories enrich the instructions so that your experience of the teachings is more holistic. (The eight-day silent retreat at which these teachings were developed did just that. Each day a spiritual talk on one contemplative attitude complemented one instructional topic.) If you are reading Part I and find your mind overburdened by instructions, I recommend dipping into Part II until you feel ready to return to the instructions in Part I. Also, because Part I provides increasingly subtle instructions on contemplative practice, you may find some chapters of Part I more meaningful for your current way of prayer than other chapters. Let the Holy Spirit and your intuition be your guide.

Who Will Find This Book Useful

I offer this in-depth exploration of the sacred symbols and the contemplative attitudes in the hope that they will help the long-term centering prayer practitioner work in subtle ways on advanced issues. However, the book is also designed to support the beginning practitioner and those who have longed for some kind of wordless meditation practice and are only just discovering that one exists within the Christian tradition.

Although the instructions in this book are set in the context of the Christian tradition, meditators in other traditions may find that the contemplative attitudes and practices shed light on their own practice. I hope that by writing in both Christian theological terms and the language of consciousness I have made the practice of centering prayer accessible to both those who are deeply rooted in the Christian tradition and to serious seekers in other traditions.

I invite you into an exploration t̶ contemplative practice now and thro̶ spiritual journey.

PART I

Deepening Your
Centering Prayer Practice
in the Light of Contemplation

CHAPTER ONE

Understanding Christian Contemplation and Getting Started in Centering Prayer

Be still and know that I am God.

—Psalm 46:10

If you asked me for just one bit of advice about contemplation, I would say to practice the meaning of one word: *amen*. If you asked me how you could meditate, how you should relate to God, how you might pray, I would whisper, "Amen." If I remember only one simple thing at the end of my own life, I hope it will be *amen*.

"Amen" is used in the Western religions to express profound faith, to assent to Mystery, to surrender to God. In the Christian tradition, "amen" is the one word that ends every prayer in words, including the words of the Lord's Prayer, the Our Father. Amen means, literally, "so be it" or "let it be." After any petition or prayer, "amen" is the *so be it,* the *let it be* that releases that prayer or petition into God, with a radical trust that nothing more needs to be said, nothing else needs to be done.

With amen, your words and actions yield to God's presence. Amen doesn't mean being passive; it doesn't mean that you do not act in the face of injustice. Amen means trusting that you can't confront injustice on your own, that you need to let your own, self-initiated efforts and agenda be, in God. With the deep surrender of amen you are more aligned with God, the source of freer and more sustained action. As you say "amen," as you practice *so be it,* God takes over. As you practice amen, God is with you in all that you do, including your actions to confront injustice. In Christianity, *amen*—"so be it," "let it be"—expresses the spirit of contemplative prayer, or contemplation.

Contemplative Practice: The Prayer in Secret

The two-thousand-year-old Christian contemplative tradition recognizes that in order to radically trust in a reality that you cannot see, you need to prepare yourself through actions, disciplines, and practices whose purpose, quite simply, is to bring you more easily to amen.

Knowledge of how to practice contemplation in Christianity has ebbed and flowed over the centuries and became nearly lost in the modern and postmodern eras. Different contemplative teachers throughout the centuries have shown how, in the Christian scriptures, Jesus instructed his followers to pray with an inner focus, a hiddenness, and a commitment to God alone. Jesus said, "When you pray, go to your inner room, close the door, and pray to your Father in secret. And your Father who sees in secret will reward you" (Matthew 6:6).[1] Contemplative teachers throughout the centuries interpret Jesus's teaching on how to pray symbolically rather than literally. Father Laurence Freeman writes, "As a private room would have been a great luxury in Jesus' time, his focus is not so much on domestic arrangements as on the orientation of the mind and heart at the time of prayer."[2] That "prayer in secret" is what later Christians called contemplation.

But rather than leaving his followers detailed instructions in scripture about how to practice the prayer in secret, Jesus gave his followers his resurrected life, his indwelling presence, the Christ consciousness that is the source of Christian contemplation. For a Christian seeker, this consciousness is everything. Illuminated by the reality of "the Mind of Christ" (1 Corinthians 2:16), the living God who comes into consciousness and ordinary life not as an object of fundamentalist belief or an exclusivist savior, Christianity becomes a transformative path. Following this path requires practice. In scripture, the apostle Paul speaks of the need for practice when he says we are to "be transformed by the renewing of your minds" (Romans 12:2).

Touched by the resurrected life of Christ, the first Christian contemplatives whose oral teachings on contemplative practice were written down became known as the desert fathers and desert mothers, the *abbas* and *ammas*. One third-century desert father, Abba Isaac, is quoted as saying:

> We need to be especially careful to follow the Gospel pre-
> cepts which instruct us to go into our room and shut the
> door so that we may pray to our Father and this is how we
> can do it. We pray in our room whenever we withdraw
> our hearts completely from the tumult and the noise of our
> thoughts and our worries, and when secretly and intimately
> we offer our prayers to the Lord . . . . [W]e pray in secret
> when in our hearts alone and in our recollected spirits . . . we
> must pray in utter silence.[3]

Abba Isaac offered his own way of withdrawing from thoughts and worries, a way of praying in silence and in secrecy that began with repeating a phrase from scripture. Since the time of the desert fathers and desert mothers, other teachers and other communities of con-templative practitioners have offered their own ways of practice.[4]

At some point, all contemplative practices end with the attitude of amen—so be it, let it be—radical consent to receiving God. That is the *reward* of the interiority, the secrecy, the living relationship with God of which Jesus spoke.

Centering Prayer: Consenting to Amen

Even though the God that Jesus reveals is ever-present, in the beginning it is hard to consent directly to the divine life within. The prayer in secret may seem a little too concealed! You need a simple practice to help you, a way of opening to the gift of God. A good contemplative practice makes you more present to the divine presence in you and aligns your actions with the divine action in you. As your contemplative practice opens you to the divine within, you also experience how the divine is present and acting in your meditation and prayer and in all of life.

Centering prayer, as taught by Thomas Keating and the organization he founded, Contemplative Outreach, is a very simple yet profound contemplative practice that orients you on the path toward transformation in Christ. The basic guidelines are:

1. Choose a sacred word as the symbol of your intention to consent to God's presence and action within.

2. Sitting comfortably and with eyes closed, settle briefly and silently introduce the sacred word as the symbol of your consent to God's presence and action within.

3. When engaged with your thoughts (which include body sensations, feelings, images, and reflections), return ever so gently to the sacred word.

4. At the end of the prayer period, remain in silence with eyes closed for a couple of minutes.

These basic instructions on centering prayer, found in Keating's classic handbook *Open Mind, Open Heart,* are a foundation for the entire spiritual journey. They reduce the obstacles to Jesus's prayer in secret, which is the gift of contemplation. They are also the infrastructure for the ways of deepening centering prayer described in this book. On this solid foundation you can build a well-grounded contemplative practice that serves you for your complete spiritual journey, as your relationship with God develops and becomes more subtle. As you practice the path of centering prayer, your experience of God deepens. God is not just a transcendent truth outside you, but a living reality within you, a mystery, a hidden ground from which everything in life is born, in every moment of time.

Chapter 2 explores the wisdom and beauty of these guidelines in more depth, giving those new to centering prayer a solid introduction. It also invites longtime practitioners to renew their foundation in centering prayer by revisiting the wealth of meaning contained in these four simple guidelines. It looks specifically at ways to reconnect with guidelines 1, 2, and 4. The material in Part II, on the contemplative attitudes, will help you enter more deeply into the third guideline, which is about what you actually do during the period of centering prayer: *when engaged with your thoughts, return ever so gently to the sacred word.*

As centering prayer unfolds, your actions affect your receptivity. For example, when you act *gently* in centering prayer, you become more open to *effortlessly* receiving God. Likewise, your receptivity affects your actions. When you recognize and experience how being *effortless* helps you rest in contemplation, it is easier for you to return *gently* to your sacred word during centering prayer. Thus, there are very subtle and very receptive ways that you can practice contemplation, and all are built on the foundation of the basic guidelines of centering prayer. And because God is ever-present in you, your beginning actions in centering prayer are already infused with the fullness of grace. Centering prayer and contemplation are not so separate when you align yourself with God in centering prayer and when you have a skillful way of practicing the subtleties of contemplation.

States, Stages, and Seasons of Contemplation

The contemplative path first includes temporary experiences of a deepening relationship with God and then more enduring stages in which you abide more fully and continuously in that relationship. Having the temporary experiences, opened to you in centering prayer, orients you to what a deeper relationship of union and unity is like. The temporary *state* is also the beginning of the longer journey toward the enduring, abiding *stage,* but, as the philosopher of consciousness Ken Wilber says, should not be mistaken for this more permanent condition.[5] Abiding in the deeper *stages* of the spiritual journey and the relationship with God requires more than experiencing a temporary *state,* like the way living in oneness with your spouse requires much more than your first passionate kiss.

As you will see, this book describes four ways to deepen your practice of centering prayer and open you to four deepening states of contemplation—four deeper and more subtle ways of experiencing God. I have found that centering prayer practitioners are sometimes drawn to whichever one of the four ways of deepening centering prayer that reflects the stage of the spiritual journey they are in. But none of the ways to use the teachings in this book requires you to figure out which spiritual stage you are in. You can practice with one of the sacred symbols simply because you are attracted to that expression of centering prayer.

Each of the practices in the rest of Part I and the contemplative attitudes in Part II help you relate to God during any state or any stage of the spiritual journey. Knowing that your relationship with God changes and that you can learn ways of skillfully responding to these changes keeps you from getting stuck in a spiritual dark night, searching for a sense of God that is too dualistic for the way God is now really present to you. Trusting God, the true teacher of prayer, to guide you in the ways these teachings best benefit your practice is what is most important.

Because distinguishing between states and stages of contemplation is a complex issue, often best left for contemplative spiritual direction, in this book I will primarily use the metaphor of spiritual seasons rather than the language of states and stages.[6] The seasons of the year unfold in linear time, yet recur in different ways, as an organic cycle, every year. Each of the four seasons has its own richness, challenges, and natural attraction for different people. Learning how to open to the richness of life in this moment, with God, whatever the season, is what the teachings in this book are about.

How do you "get to" union with God? Practice, practice, practice—continuously, skillfully, and in deepening appreciation for the subtle mystery of divine love.

CHAPTER TWO

Renewing Your Practice of Centering Prayer

He is like the man who when he built his house dug,
and dug deep, and laid the foundation on rock; when
the river was in flood it bore down on that house but
could not shake it, it was so well built.

—Luke 6:48[1]

Let's look in this chapter at how valuable the centering prayer basic guidelines are, even for longtime practitioners. Many of the difficulties encountered by longtime practitioners are helped by returning to the simple wealth of meaning that is contained in the four introductory guidelines.

For example, a woman whom I will call Jane was meeting with me in spiritual direction. Jane had been practicing centering prayer for about eight years. She told me, "I am still doing my centering prayer every day, but it's sometimes hard to get to my prayer spot. I don't feel as motivated as I once did. I don't sense Jesus's presence like before. I sometimes feel spacey during prayer and ungrounded in life. What can I do?"

Jane's symptoms are not all that unusual for an advancing practitioner of centering prayer. She had an established discipline of daily prayer and had regularly gone on annual intensive retreats. As a result, her contemplative relationship with God was deepening, and she was being invited to go deeper with her practice. I immediately saw that the things she was describing were symptoms of a deeper condition. This is a situation that she could do something about. Symptoms like lack of motivation and spaciness or lack of groundedness in life sometimes happen in longtime practitioners of centering prayer, but most may not know how to respond. Jane found that going back to the basics of centering prayer helped her recover a freshness of practice. By doing so, she attuned herself to the new life that God was bringing forth in her.

Reviving Your Motivation by Renewing Your Intention and Consent

Reconnect with the first basic guideline: *choose a sacred word as the symbol of your intention to consent to God's presence and action within.*

Jane and I began by exploring her diminished motivation for the spiritual journey. Problems often arise when you no longer feel the same enthusiasm for the spiritual journey that you once did. It is often disconcerting when your relationship with God changes. Spiritual honeymoons change. If you perceive a hidden invitation to growth within the change, the relationship deepens. If you cannot perceive that invitation, you may end the relationship. Centering prayer opens us to a deeper, but also a more subtle relationship with God. Conceptually understanding this shift helps, but more helpful is bringing your understanding into your practice every day. Most valuable is translating your conceptual understanding into experience by consenting to the growth in the relationship.

Motivation has to do with intention: *why* you are doing what you are doing. As we are drawn toward greater oneness with Christ, our intention and our consent need to be refined to reflect a relationship that is less dualistic. When we attune and renew our intention, then our motivation for the spiritual journey is reaffirmed and deepened.

I asked Jane how she was preparing herself for her period of centering prayer and what she understood her sacred word to mean. She said, "Why, I just sit down and begin by starting to say my sacred word. I chose it long ago and don't really think about it anymore."

During the practice of centering prayer, it is essential not to think about the meaning of your sacred word. But there is a way you can renew the intention behind the sacred word so that your motivation for continuing on the spiritual path deepens when your relationship with God changes. Recall how the first of centering prayer's basic guidelines says that the sacred word is sacred because it expresses your *intention to consent to God's presence and action.* When your prayer no longer feels sacred, one thing you can do as a longtime practitioner is utilize the preparatory time before formally beginning centering prayer by taking a moment to renew your intention, the *why* of your practice. As you affirm the new and deeper meaning for your prayer, let your sacred word express a renewed consent to God's presence and action.

Some married couples have discovered that renewing their wedding vows every year, in light of their changing relationship, helps deepen their marriage. Once in a while, they practice bringing to mind the changes and newness in their relationship. Then they consent to this new relationship by applying their insights in everyday life, bringing the original "I do" to new meaning and renewing their motivation. Your relationship with God invites a similar practice.

Here are three possible ways that renewing your intention in centering prayer might take shape for you, depending on the way your contemplative prayer is developing:

- *Before the time of centering prayer,* you reflect on who or what God is for you at this time of your spiritual journey. Then, with this sense of meaning in your conscious mind, you let your sacred symbol come to you as a nonreflective way of consenting to this more personal sense of God's presence.

- Your reflections may show you that at this time God is a mystery whom you do not or cannot consciously know. That's not a problem for practice. As you realize or remember that God is an unknowable mystery and join this realization in your mind with your sacred word, you infuse your practice with an intention that expresses the truth of your relationship with God. Your intention becomes opening to mystery itself.

- Perhaps when you reflect on who or what God is, you find that you are spiritually dry and resistant even to opening to a mystery you no can no longer conceive of. This is still not necessarily a problem when your intention is vast and nuanced. For in these situations, your intention can be to simply surrender yourself to the unknown. Remember, in centering prayer you are saying yes both to God's presence and God's action. God's action includes the purification and transformation of your idea of who God is, your felt ability to say yes to God, and sometimes even your capacity to pray. In the unknowing, the pure consent and the surrender of your ability to pray, you are brought to deep receptivity, so that the Spirit prays in you.

Over the next months, Jane began utilizing the preparatory period for centering prayer more consciously. Each day she prepared for her centering prayer by reflecting on or just remembering for a moment who God was for her now. God was no longer being revealed to her through the felt presence of Jesus. Rather, God was an unknowable mystery. Then she let her sacred word come to her as a way of consenting to this aspect of God. As she continued, she realized she also felt some sadness about the change in her relationship, some grief about Jesus's felt absence. So she learned to introduce her sacred word at the beginning of centering prayer with greater meaning, as a way of saying yes to God's healing action. Again, this exercise of reflecting on the context for her practice of centering prayer happened before her centering prayer began, as a preparation for it. But for Jane, it was an important preparation. As she brought the truth of who God really was to mind every day and then said yes to this truth through her sacred word, she began to accept and respond to God.

Then she continued in the nonconceptual consent to God's presence and action that is at the heart of centering prayer. Rather than thinking about God, she just said yes to God, through returning to her sacred word. But now her sacred word was blessed with the deeper reality of who God was for her. When honesty comes into a relationship, deeper truths are possible. Jane's intention, the *why* of her prayer, was now about relating to who God was for her, not who God wasn't. God received her consent and in turn gave Jane great joy in the unknown. Her motivation for the spiritual journey was brought back to life as she aligned her centering prayer with God. Coming back to a fresh understanding and practice of the first basic guideline on the context for centering prayer—intention and consent—was what helped her.

You don't need a clear sense all the time of who or what God is to be doing the practice correctly. If you are already well established on the contemplative path, with a well-formed discipline in daily life and on retreat, and you experience resistance to doing centering prayer, you may be in the midst of a process in which

God replaces your own self-generated reasons for meditating with a purer intention. Too often you may get hung up on seeking tangible experiences of Jesus's presence or even looking for tangible effects in daily life. At such times, the divine life is infusing your prayer life with a more profound meaning. If, as a longtime practitioner, your motivation changes or even seems to disappear, remember that you are being invited to rely on a purer, gifted motivation, freer from self-reference. God gives you this deeper, selfless motivation for the spiritual journey. Renewing your intention and then consenting to God's action transforms not only your idea of who or what God is, but also your self-referential reasons for pursuing the spiritual journey. Reducing the self-referencing helps you transform your motivation for following the whole contemplative path into selfless union with Christ and unity in God's emergence in all of life.

How Your Body Position Affects Your Inner Posture During Prayer

Reconnect to the second basic guideline: *sitting comfortably and with eyes closed, settle briefly and silently introduce the sacred word as the symbol of your consent to God's presence and action within.*

I asked Jane about the physical posture she used during centering prayer. She told me, "I have a recliner chair at home that I sit in. With my head back on the cushion, I feel very relaxed. Sometimes I doze off. The comfortable chair helps me lose awareness of my body."

Her posture helped explain the spaciness she felt in prayer. Contemplative resting in God can bring physical relaxation. However, resting in God is primarily an *inner* resting of your being in God's Being. The receptivity needed to deepen centering prayer is facilitated by having a body position that is alert and attentive.

Unless you have a physical condition that requires special care, being so comfortable in your chair that you lose awareness of your body often leads to a kind of spaciness that, although temporarily relaxing, is not as valuable as contemplation. In contemplation, God's indwelling presence normally manifests through spiritual attentiveness, as awareness is transformed in you. Realizing God's indwelling presence in pure awareness is much more valuable spiritually than feeling relaxed or losing awareness.

But you also don't want a posture that is rigid or constrained. Centering prayer's effects are very ordinary, sometimes hidden in daily life and certainly unseen during your own self-reflection. During prayer, having a natural, upright body posture that is not special or unique is very helpful. Some people find that kneeling or sitting cross-legged on the floor, even in a full lotus position, brings them inner alertness. But for many people, kneeling or sitting in lotus position is too constraining, too tight, too unnatural a position for centering prayer.

Our inner posture before God is affected by our outer bodily posture. Cultivate alert responsiveness on the outside and the inside. If you find that you are spacey or, alternatively, tight, constrained, and rigid in your prayer, remember the basic guideline about physical posture. As Jane regained the sense of having a comfortable, alert posture in prayer, her spaciness dissipated.

Grounding Your Centering Prayer Practice by Letting Intention and Consent Flow into Your Life

Reconnect to the fourth basic guideline: *at the end of the prayer period, remain in silence with eyes closed for a couple of minutes.*

As Jane's spaciness and lack of motivation for the spiritual journey shifted, we turned to her final and most important issue: being "ungrounded in life." I asked her to describe more fully what she meant by this phrase. She said, "I used to feel invigorated in my life as a result of my centering prayer. Now I feel a little more inward, less rooted in the world. I know this isn't good because prayer should bring me back to others. So I feel bad about that."

Although a sense of inwardness and detachment from the world often develops with the spiritual journey, Jane's concern about being ungrounded in life was a valuable self-insight. Being ungrounded is different from being detached. So once again, Jane and I explored how the basic foundational guidelines of centering prayer could help her align herself with a deepened experience of God. I asked her how she was ending her prayer periods.

"Well," she said, "I just let go of my sacred word and then get up. I know I am supposed to sit there for a moment, so I try to. But usually I just start thinking about my day, so I may just as well get to it. I don't feel that peaceful anyway."

The fourth beginning guideline for centering prayer says, "At the end of the prayer period, remain in silence with eyes closed for a couple of minutes." Just as the preparatory minutes for centering prayer are an important time, in which you can use prayers in words, your thoughts about God, or reading scripture to briefly get in touch with an intention that disposes you for the ensuing period when you are not to be concerned about thoughts, the concluding period provides an important opportunity for you to return to prayers in words, your thoughts, or reading scripture. Just as the preparatory minutes allow you to establish your intention of faith and relationship with God for the actual period of centering prayer, the concluding minutes help you reemerge into ordinary life with an intention that is more rooted in God. These additional minutes enable you to bring the atmosphere of silence into everyday life.

Jane and I spoke about five things she could do to conclude her centering prayer well and create a bridge between prayer and activity. First, we explored how she might spend a few moments just resting in God. In the same way that you should not immediately slam your car into fifth gear after it has been in reverse, in centering prayer, you should take a moment to rest your mind and heart and be in the present moment after you have let go of the sacred word. By letting go of effort and just resting, you allow the relational quality of the prayer to enfold any lingering sense of self-achievement there might be in you. Similar to the way you might conclude lovemaking by resting in the arms of your beloved in order to remain in the union that is beyond and within physical pleasure, you conclude centering prayer by taking time to rest in God without trying to find God, without even trying to meditate. You really learn receptivity in relationship when you let go of all activity, when you let go of the sacred word, and simply be.

As Jane began taking time to rest in God at the conclusion of her centering prayer, she realized how hard she been trying with her sacred word. When she ended her centering prayer period the way she had previously, sometimes her mind was full of thoughts. But now she learned to just be, in the hiddenness of faith, and simply rest in the ordinary moment with everything, including God, amidst thoughts. The experience of not using the sacred word at the conclusion of her centering prayer gave her a greater sense of how to use it during centering prayer: with receptivity rather than effort.

I also encouraged Jane to explore a second bridge between her centering prayer and resuming activity. After resting her mind in openness in the first moments after letting go of her sacred word, she took another moment to bring her mind and attention to her sense perceptions. She noticed her breathing and gently directed her attention throughout her body, sensing her face, neck, arms, back, legs, and feet. Focusing on her body helped her ground the effects of centering prayer in her sensory experience. She began to experience how sensation naturally arises and falls in awareness. Sometimes she became more aware of the tension she was feeling about her upcoming day. As she let her attention rest in the tension, blessed by the effects of her centering prayer, the sensation released a bit.

In the wake of grace, everything finds its natural release. The inner anxiety behind physical tension often dissipates when, after centering prayer, you embrace God by gently resting your attention in the tension and anxiety. In centering prayer, you open yourself to resting in God's presence in pure awareness. Pure awareness is the ground in which all specific sensations and perceptions arise and fall. Integrating this resting in pure awareness with attention to sense perception is a way of bridging the secrecy of centering prayer and manifest life. When Jane ended her prayer in this way, she found that she was more grounded, more attentive, during the day.

Thirdly, I suggested that Jane might offer the centering prayer period that she had just finished to someone in need. She might choose a specific person she knew to be ill or suffering or find a more general situation in the world—such as hunger, social injustice, or the degradation of the environment—with which she might unite her own spiritual journey. By offering her prayer for the needs of others, she would practice giving up the sense of self-focus that affects some people on the spiritual journey if they are not sensitive to the needs of the world around them. We do need times apart from the needs of the world to pray, as the gospels show Jesus himself doing. However, offering your silent prayer for the needs of the world brings you into the central insight of Jesus's teaching and life: you are not separate from others. The spiritual journey does not take place in isolation from others.

Jane found that as she concluded her prayer in this way, over time the natural effects of centering prayer, union with Christ and unity with others in God, flowed more easily into her life. When you surrender that which is most dear to you—the beauty and meaning of your spiritual journey—you really penetrate the mystery of sacrifice and open to union with Christ. Contemplation is not a self-focused activity.

A fourth way of bridging centering prayer and activity is, after letting go of your sacred symbol and resting your mind for a moment, to briefly visualize a scene from your coming day. Let your sacred symbol return to you while you visualize this event, as a way of blessing the day with the effects of your centering prayer. Then let the symbol go, along with the imagined scene.

A fifth way of creating a bridge from centering prayer to activity is to use the concluding moments to say or listen to the Lord's Prayer. The simple sentences of the Lord's Prayer contain a wealth of meaning. We will explore the way that this prayer is the capstone of Jesus's teaching on contemplation, the prayer in secret, in Chapter 8. Entering into a prayer in words, especially the Lord's Prayer, after centering prayer allows you to begin integrating silence and words, interior silence and thoughts, contemplative prayer and other prayers, the divine life within you and the human world around you.

I am not saying you should follow all of these suggestions. Instead, use those that allow you to renew your practice in a way appropriate to your own situation. Jane, for example, was drawn to practicing the second and third suggestions. At the conclusion of her centering prayer, she brought her attention to her breath and body and then prayed for others. Afterward, during activity, she found she was more grounded in her body. After offering her centering prayer for the needs of the undocumented immigrants in her area, whose situation she did not sympathize with politically, she found herself being more compassionate and connected to everyone around her.

These five suggestions are not the only ways of bridging centering prayer with activity. Choose one or two, or use them as inspiration for building your own bridge between prayer and activity.

Growth on the spiritual journey comes when the divine life within us, which we need only receive, breaks into our conscious experience, changing the structures of our consciousness and even, as we will see, changing the way we experience and relate to God. Let your exploration of the subtleties of centering prayer practice flow from God's life within, opened by practicing the basic guidelines of centering prayer.

CHAPTER THREE

Deepening the Sacred Word

In returning and rest you shall be saved;
in quietness and trust shall be your strength.
— Isaiah 30:15

The basic guidelines of centering prayer are usually given in relationship with a word of one or two syllables, a sacred word. However, as Thomas Keating says in *Open Mind, Open Heart* and in the foreword to this book, you may instead choose for your practice other forms of the sacred symbol: your breath or a glance. There is also a fourth way of practicing centering prayer: with no symbol, no "thing" as an intermediary in your prayer between you and God—the sacred nothingness.

Whichever symbol you choose, by practicing with it, you consent to the presence and action of God. God's presence and action come alive, *become conscious,* in your prayer through the intention with which you pray, through your repeated practice and, of course, through grace. Yet in centering prayer's basic instructions not much is said about how contemplation deepens when you practice with the different symbols or about how God's presence that comes to life in contemplation affects the deepening practice of centering prayer. There are similarities in the ways of practicing with each of the symbols, yet there are also different benefits to practicing with each of them.

The following chapters on the sacred word, the sacred breath, the sacred glance, and the sacred nothingness teach how, when, and why to practice with these sacred symbols, so that your relationship with God deepens and so that you are not stuck in one way of doing centering prayer that may no longer reflect what your relationship with God really is. Each symbol, when practiced in the right way, helps you relate to God during the different seasons of the spiritual journey, in ways unique to who you are, and during the challenges that arise on the spiritual path. These chapters will bring out nuances that may help you during different seasons of your spiritual journey. When developed rightly, each sacred symbol yields its fruits: a fuller relationship with Christ, more inner freedom, and the ability to be of greater service to others.

The approach presented in this chapter brings to life the deeper dynamics of contemplation that open once you have established your commitment to daily centering prayer practice. Exploring these dynamics is valuable whether you are practicing centering prayer with the sacred word, using another symbol, or following another style of meditation.

Moving from Rigidity to Receptivity

The primary obstacle to deepening centering prayer in the first years of practice is rigidity. Rigidity develops unconsciously, especially when you are caught in the attitude that centering prayer is something that you are doing on your own. There is an important difference between a technique and prayer. A technique is something you learn and do on your own that yields predictable results. If you do A and B, then you can expect to get C.

Prayer, on the other hand, is learned and practiced, but is always done in relationship with God. With God, we never know what to expect. There are things you need to do, but you also allow yourself to be undone. Through your actions you are brought to receptivity. In turn, you let receptivity inform your actions. You learn to say and be amen, so be it. In so doing, you receive God's light, love, and life. Deepening the sacred word in centering prayer is about recognizing centering prayer as prayer and about letting God become the source, the means, and the end, more and more, of your contemplative life. The Spirit becomes intertwined with your own actions. As you experience this interweaving consciously in your practice, you realize that you are not alone in prayer. As you go deeper, you lose the conscious awareness of how grace and your actions in meditation combine in your prayer. Then God's presence and action awaken more and more in your life.

What are some of the common symptoms of rigidity that come up in the first few years of doing centering prayer? We get caught grinding away on the sacred word. We try to use the sacred word to battle against thoughts. We unconsciously hammer on the sacred word in our mind. We try so hard, and in our trying, find that God is far away from us. We hope that the sacred word, if we use it just right, will get us to God.

Anyone can get caught in self-conscious efforts to do the method right. This concern about technique can lead you into attitudes of not only rigidity, but also resistance, effort, achievement, strategizing, repression, and separation. These attitudes are anything but contemplative. They keep you trapped on the surface of prayer, left alone with the external form of your sacred word.

When you learn to pray through the sacred word, with God, you develop contemplative attitudes that have a very different feeling from the rigid, technique-oriented attitudes named above. These attitudes will be brought to life in Part II of this book, but for the moment you can get a sense of their contemplative feeling from their names: receiving, consent, simplicity, gentleness, letting go, resting, embracing, and integrating. As you practice in these contemplative attitudes, you realize what Isaiah means in scripture when he says, "In returning and rest you shall be saved; in quietness and trust shall be your strength" (Isaiah 30:15). These contemplative attitudes are simply ways of resting in the living Word of God in your prayer in quietness and trust rather than in effort and rigidity. You let go of technique, effort, and separation as you let the sacred word deepen in you. This chapter describes simple ways of doing just that. But a note of caution here: rather than "doing" what this chapter describes, settle gently into the shift in consciousness invited by these pages. Let your deep intuition affirm the rest within your returning in prayer; let God bring forth the strength of quietness and trust in your life. In other words, don't try to do it on your own.

In the contemplative attitudes, with God as your partner, you learn and relearn how to relate to the sacred word. The sacred word is not a vehicle that gets you to God. The sacred word is a symbol of your intention to consent to the presence and action of God. Deepening the sacred word in centering prayer creates greater space for God to come to life in your conscious experience of prayer. You have to learn and relearn receptivity, amen, so be it, over and over again. The process of being brought, in the first years of the spiritual journey, from technique to true prayer establishes you in a living relationship with Christ. Your identity shifts; you discover a new sense of who you are, a new life, in the deepening relationship of prayer.

After learning this material on a retreat, one longtime centering prayer practitioner told me that it was only now that she really understood centering prayer. I asked her what she meant. She said that as she experienced a new way of relating to her sacred word and to God, she finally realized, "Now I am a contemplative." This realization showed her how trapped she used to be in a self-isolating focus on technique. Her old patterns of activity and the sense of identity associated with them were now enfolded by a deeper realization. Now, she was not alone in her practice. Her description expresses the interior shift in the sense of identity, the sense of who you are, that allows you to make the hard choices involved with changing your life. Knowing your true life in God, who you really are, helps you make contemplative values the focus of life. Deepening the sacred word in centering prayer helps you change and be changed on the contemplative path, from the inside out.

The Word Returns to You

In practicing centering prayer with the sacred word, the workings of your mind, which are so conditioned to thinking about thoughts in the wonderful human gift of self-reflection, shift in grace into a new way of being. In scripture Paul recommends, "Let the same mind be in you that was in Christ Jesus" (Philippians 2:5). The Mind of Christ is not a mind of information, not a mind of intellectual ability, not a mind of knowing. The Mind of Christ involves direct experience, unmediated by intellectual thought. The Mind of Christ is a mind of contemplative faith. Contemplation, because it is a nonconceptual form of prayer, opens you to a deeper, experiential form of faith, a way of unknowing consent, in which God comes alive in your prayer. You put on, or receive, the Mind of Christ.

Christian mystical theology speaks of two forms of contemplation: acquired contemplation and infused contemplation. In acquired contemplation, your actions predominate in prayer; you attain some sense of God through what you do. In infused contemplation, God's presence and action predominate; everything about the prayer is a pure gift. In a way, a good contemplative practice simply trains you to receive the grace of infused contemplation as your actions are aligned more and more with God in acquired contemplation. In deepening the sacred word in centering prayer, the way you learn how to relate to your sacred word trains you to let the living Word of God act in you. The distinction between acquired and infused contemplation is lessened over time, especially when you practice in contemplative attitudes like gentleness, letting go, and resting. The approach we are reinforcing is a simple way, flowing forth from the foundation of the basic guidelines of centering prayer, for acquiring infused contemplation, for letting the living Word of God pray in you through your deepening relationship with your sacred word.

Your sacred word becomes a symbol of consent to the living Word of God in you. Rigidity is useless in relating with the living God. It is the Logos, the life-giving Word, the Christ, to which you relate in deepening contemplation. You begin to learn how to relate with the living Word through your skillful, receptive way of relating to your sacred word in centering prayer. In deepening the sacred word in centering prayer, you experience how the sacred word comes to you out of the Mind of Christ, and you learn to let go of your sacred word in order to rest in what could be called God's Sacred Word. The essential disposition for deepening the sacred word in centering prayer is, when engaged with your thoughts, let the sacred word ever so gently return to you.

When you learn a new way of relating to the sacred word in centering prayer, you learn a new way of relating to your thoughts. When you move out of technique and effort and make space for God between you and your sacred word, God comes to life in you in a real way, and a new inner spaciousness begins to develop between you and all thoughts.

The fruit of deepening the sacred word in centering prayer is an introductory form of contemplative prayer—similar to what

Saint Teresa of Avila calls the "prayer of recollection"—in which your thoughts are recollected in the Mind of Christ. When your thoughts are recollected in this state of contemplative prayer, you are not identified with them; you begin to discover a new sense of who you are and what your inner life is like. Thomas Keating says, "The occasional experience of freedom from attachment to thoughts is the beginning of Contemplative Prayer in the classic sense of the term."[1] Thoughts can still be in your mind, but they are "recollected" in the deeper Mind of Christ within you. Amen, so be it, comes into your practice more and more.

The Sacred Word as Suitable for Certain Seasons of the Spiritual Journey

Deepening ways of practicing centering prayer unfold in a natural way across the seasons of the spiritual journey. The more contemplative focus of deepening the sacred word builds upon the foundation of the basic guidelines of centering prayer, moving toward more active contemplative attitudes, greater openness to God in prayer, and less rigidity. These are the qualities that help the prayer of recollection awaken in you. John of the Cross says that in the early stages of the spiritual journey, people generally go through an active phase, which he calls the "active night of sense." Deepening the sacred word in centering prayer can be especially helpful during the active night of sense. In this season of the contemplative path, you are called to make actions that direct and discipline your mind, senses, and emotions, as well as your external lifestyle, to God.

In this season of the spiritual journey, you are letting your way of thinking be changed by God into a new way of being. This new inner way of being, putting on the Mind of Christ, begins to change your way of being in life. The daily practice of centering prayer initiates the inner changes, as you open to the first deepening state of contemplation, the prayer of recollection, and experience a new relationship with your thoughts. The first great inner task in the beginning of centering prayer is letting your consciousness be formed to and by the contemplative attitudes we will explore in detail in Part II. In deepening the sacred word in centering prayer, you practice attitudes such as simplicity, gentleness, letting go, and resting in God. The Mind of Christ comes to life in you, along with these attitudes.

The second task at the beginning of the spiritual journey is more external: making contemplation the central value of your life. Contemplative monks and nuns make contemplation the central value of their external lives by leaving the world and entering a monastery or convent. If you are not a monk or nun, you "leave" your old life not by going to a monastery, but by making contemplative practice the fulcrum of your day, in a new lifestyle centered on God. In a very simple but direct way, you make contemplation the central value of your life when you sculpt time out of your schedule to practice centering prayer twice a day. But in this daily practice you are doing much more than giving up old routines and making space for new values in your life. In deepening the sacred word in centering prayer, you practice new inner habits, replacing rigidity with gentleness, technique with prayer, your separate-self sense with a living relationship with God. How you relate to your sacred word, the transparent symbol of consent to God's Sacred Word, creates more freedom inside you as you disidentify from thoughts. When you disidentify from thoughts, you learn how to disidentify from old habits in life and listen to the Spirit's invitation to a new life. You disidentify from your thoughts when your deep spiritual identity, created in the image and likeness of God, awakens within. Deepening the sacred word in centering prayer helps you during the first stage, or season, of the spiritual journey.

Most people find that going on a long, intensive retreat convinces them of the value of regular practice. After some time doing centering prayer—perhaps a year for some people, more for others—these beginning tasks are set in place, at least initially. When your interior consciousness and your external life are changed, you establish a primary commitment to the contemplative life that initiates the transformative process. New horizons open. Your experience of and relationship with God begins to deepen and develop in whole new ways. As your spiritual life develops and your relationship with God changes, you will need to return, reestablish, and renew your commitment to shifting your interior consciousness and your external life many times. Yet the work you do changing your life, and being changed in life, in the first years of your spiritual journey gives you a firm footing for these ongoing tasks.

With greater inner freedom and from a lifestyle given over to the new values of the contemplative path, you are also freer to serve others. When you are less attached to thoughts, you are liberated from the sense that you are a self forever separate from God and other people. As you let contemplation infuse your actions in centering prayer, as the life of God comes alive in you, your spiritual journey unfolds more easily, in God.

The Active Contemplative Attitudes with the Sacred Word

In order to describe more fully how to practice deepening the sacred word in centering prayer, each of the eight following sections applies one of the eight active contemplative attitudes to the sacred word: opening to God, consent, simplicity, gentleness, letting go, resting, embracing, and integrating prayer and life. The actual practice of deepening the sacred word in centering prayer is very simple. Everything you learn in centering prayer's basic guidelines remains the foundation of your contemplative practice. You just allow a freer relationship with your symbol.

The contemplative attitudes help your practice deepen by affirming how God is coming alive in this expression of centering prayer. By seeing how the contemplative attitudes apply to the sacred word, you cooperate more fully with God's presence and action in your contemplative practice. The following sections are best read as a way of supporting your ongoing practice of centering prayer.

Opening to God through the Sacred Word

The most important disposition for deepening the sacred word in centering prayer is the openhanded attitude of receptivity. You practice the attitude of opening to God in the way you relate to your sacred word. The introductory guidelines of centering prayer tell you to choose your sacred word. There isn't any great mystery about this. Your word doesn't have to appear to you in a burning bush. You don't have to feel that it was whispered to you by God. You can simply open yourself to God and choose it. Yet it is valuable to remember and renew from time to time the attitude of receptivity regarding your sacred word. Your word is sacred because you are using it in prayer. You are in relationship with God even though in centering prayer you do not rely on words, concepts, or symbols to relate with God. The way you deepen in contemplation is by being open to the living Word of God.

A good way to learn this receptivity is through your relationship with your sacred word. For example, when beginning your prayer period, it's best to not just sit down and take up your sacred word as if it were a tool for a job or a smartphone that connects you with someone you know if you just tap the right sequence of icons. Instead, take a moment to shift out of this way of being. A simple way of opening to this shift is to actually experience what it is like to open to and receive your sacred word out of the silent depths of your being—that is, instead of introducing the word yourself, see it, hear it, feel it coming to you, as if it were floating up from a deep pool of water to the surface of your mind. In the light of grace, you receive your sacred word arising from the Mind of Christ into your own conscious mind. As you practice the attitude of opening to God with your sacred word, you learn how to recognize the living Word of God. The immediate gift of recognition then infuses what you do with your sacred word as you allow greater receptivity into your practice.

Preparation for Centering Prayer: Giving God Consent to Act in You through the Sacred Word

As the basic guidelines on centering prayer suggest, when you prepare your body for the period of centering prayer, you assume a natural, easy, and open posture. In the first years on the contemplative path, closing your eyes usually helps you focus your mind. As contemplation deepens beyond the basics of centering prayer, your intention of consent is two-sided. First, trust that your practice is in relationship with God and, as you prepare for practice, take a moment to reflect on your sense of who God is for you, rather than who God is not. You may have a sense of a living relationship with God through one aspect of Christ's life—as a teacher, as one who sacrificed his life for you out of love, or as a resurrected eternal presence. Or perhaps you are relating to God's indwelling presence, beyond form or image. Call to mind your own sense of who or what the mystery of God is for you now, just as you would call your beloved by name to express the intimacy of your relationship.

Secondly, open to the mystery beyond the image, concept, sense, and form that you currently hold of who or what God is. Your practice of centering prayer leads you beyond the sacred word itself into contact with the living Word of God in interior silence, and your consent to the mystery of God is always evolving, always beckoning you beyond the current concept you have of God. Your consent to God in centering prayer is something of a paradox. You consent to both sides of God—form and mystery. The mystery of God is beyond concepts, forms, and images, yet concepts, forms, and images emerge out of this transcendent mystery to lead you deeper. Where are you led? Deeper into mystery.

Take a couple of minutes to prepare your body and mind by consenting to the living God. This preparation of your body and mind opens you to God's presence acting in you.

The Simplicity of the Sacred Word

The next five sections describe what you do during the practice period itself. Simplicity is crucial to the deepening of centering prayer. By remaining with the simplicity of the sacred word in centering prayer, without complicating the practice with other techniques or ways of prayer, contemplation deepens in you in an important way. The sacred word is a symbol that, with simple practice, goes beyond thoughts into interior silence and then, if you practice in the contemplative attitudes, integrates thoughts with interior silence. The sacred word forms your consent to mystery. Your intention to consent to the mystery of God is brought to life by returning to the sacred word when you are engaged with another thought—with every other thought.

God's presence comes into your conscious relationship with the sacred word through your simple, faithful action of returning to that word. You continue to choose, over and over again, to relate to the sacred word, by simple consent, rather than choosing to relate to thoughts, by thinking about them. In this simplicity, you are choosing to relate to the living Word of God rather than to surface thoughts about God. Centering prayer involves a very delicate form of faith, based more in unknowing and experience than in knowing and dogmatic belief. You simply return to the sacred word when you are engaged with thoughts, including thoughts about God. With this active discipline, you learn the delicate difference between thoughts and thinking about thoughts. If thoughts are flowing by and you are not engaging with them by thinking about them, you can let them go by. You open to a new form of cognition that is awakening in you, as the Mind of Christ subsumes your own intellectual mind. The simple letting go of thoughts and the more delicate letting go of thinking about thoughts opens you to deeper levels of relationship with God, in which thoughts self-release in you, without you doing anything but just being in God. The Mind of Christ becomes one with your own mind.

Gentleness with the Sacred Word

The essential instruction of centering prayer says, *When engaged with your thoughts return ever so gently to the sacred word.* As contemplation deepens, you appreciate how important the attitude of gentleness is for letting the living Word of God infuse your practice with the sacred word.

Many people struggle with the question "How can I be gentle with the sacred word?" Gentleness is something you learn and practice. You learn gentleness in centering prayer by consciously returning to the sacred word with an ease of spirit. You also learn gentleness in centering prayer by being gentle with yourself when you are effortful. And the best way to learn how to act with gentleness in prayer is to let God teach you. God is gentle. As you let go of thoughts and of thinking about thoughts, you let go of your own strategies about being gentle, and you have space in your awareness for God.

Recognize what gentleness feels like in your ordinary life: caressing your beloved, sensing a flower opening in the sunlight, picking up a newborn. Kinesthetically sense these experiences. Instead of getting trapped in your thoughts, thinking about trying to be gentle, let your experience teach you. When you are caught trying to be gentle, let go of strategies and let yourself remember, in your being, gentleness.

Don't get stuck in thoughts and strategies for how to be gentle. Then there is no need to think about being gentle during your contemplative practice. Gentleness abides in you. Let it live in your prayer, without thinking about it and without even thinking about images that evoke it.

Letting Go of the Sacred Word

As your centering prayer unfolds, you find that thoughts flow through your mind more easily. You try less. Then, as if you were in a dance and attuned to your partner's subtle guidance, you can allow another movement of the practice to unfold in you as you let the external form of the sacred word go. Let the sacred word become a whisper, a memory, a receding echo spoken by an unseen voice. Letting go of the surface form of the sacred word is a way of surrendering into the living Word of God behind and beneath and within the outer shell of the sacred word. Love is not primarily an emotion. In spiritual practice, love is an act of the will, a consent, a willingness, a letting go. If you hang onto the sacred word when God is inviting you into wordless love, you are left only with yourself. If you let God let go of the word in you, you receive divine love.

With time, you find that your contemplative practice involves less and less of your doing. You easily return to the sacred word, just being with it as it has its own life within you. As my old friend the great teacher of centering prayer Father Carl Arico has said, this is like "letting the sacred word pray you." You are no longer praying the practice, no longer praying the sacred word on your own. With your letting go, the living Word of God infuses your prayer. Learning how to recognize when God is coming into your conscious experience is very valuable in contemplation. Then all you have to do is let the divine life unfold in you, like a flower opening, on its own.

Resting in the Sacred Word of God

There is a subtle difference between letting go and resting. Resting is more intimate, more delicate than letting go. Rest in God beyond the form, the sound, the thought, and even the memory of the sacred word.

You can experience this rest in two ways. In the first, all of a sudden you realize that you were not thinking but resting in God, like when you wake up after having fallen asleep. At that time, when you consciously reflect on what has occurred, just rest your mind with all that is happening in you, as if you put your head back down on the pillow after waking.

You may be conscious that you are leaning toward rest. Your tendency may be to try to rest in God. Trying to rest in God makes God a dualistic goal. Rather, the second way of experiencing rest involves learning to rest from seeking God—rest from trying, rest from returning to God at all. This kind of resting from seeking God is like giving up trying to get to sleep. Let go of the seeking, and let rest come to you. You are now opening to the deeper meaning of Isaiah's invitation: "In returning and rest you shall be saved. In quietness and trust shall be your strength." Rest your mind from everything that is happening in you and around you so that "God may be all in all" (1 Corinthians 15:28). Nothing is excluded from the love of God—even your thoughts and your efforts to rest in God. Your commitment to the attitude of rest opens you to being; your experiences of just being in God show you how to rest.

Embracing Feelings as Your Sacred Word

Sometimes even after the experience of resting in God, you can experience strong feelings during your prayer. There is an understandable desire to want to get beyond them or get rid of them. You may find yourself resisting or repressing anger, sadness, or fear because they are painful, they bother you, they feel like obstacles to your relationship with God. In Christianity these are called the *afflictive* emotions. You may find yourself using your sacred word like a baseball bat, trying to send the feelings away from you. You may feel lost from God, overwhelmed in emotion, or perhaps just simply irritated and lost in thoughts. Returning to the sacred word at this time can be an unconscious way of repressing and avoiding feelings, especially if you are returning with effort and an unconscious attitude of resistance.

Actually, as your conscious relationship with God deepens, everything is included in your union—feelings and emotions, too. The great Benedictine abbot Dom John Chapman wrote, "When we realize that God is not only in every external event, but in every internal event—I mean in every involuntary feeling we have—we realize that, at every moment of our life, we are in touch with God."[2] Radical transformation in Christ comes when you find God in all things, including your emotions. Resisting feelings keeps you from this transformation.

Instead of returning to your sacred word outside the feeling, embrace strong feelings *as* your sacred word. Let go of returning to the thought of the sacred word and just feel the feeling, or even a corner of it, as one simple physical sensation in your bodily awareness. Let go of the form of the word in your mind and let God come through the feeling in your bodily awareness. Trust that the Spirit is acting in the feeling, to transform you and your relationship with your feelings. In the deepening of contemplation, your feelings are being freed when you make the delicate movement, in response to God's healing and transforming action, to embrace God.

It is sometimes difficult to embrace feelings as your sacred word in centering prayer, but doing so is a very valuable way to learn to cooperate with God in the transformation of your consciousness and your actions. Through the attitude of embracing you open yourself, consenting to the further mystery of God's embrace of you and your suffering.

Integrating Your Practice into Your Life

As your practice period ends, let go of returning to the sacred word and just rest your mind for a minute or two. Many people who do this find that these brief moments at the end of the practice period are the most spacious ones of their prayer. This is a sign that they were trying too hard and becoming rigid with the sacred word during the period itself. That's all right. It is just an invitation to open yourself to God, to renew yourself in the contemplative attitudes before, during, and after your next practice period.

The point of centering prayer is to integrate your periods of sitting prayer practice with activity and to realize your unity, in God, with everyone and everything in life through ordinary service. Take some time, even a minute, to offer your period of prayer for the needs of others, as described in Chapter 2. A specific concern may come to your mind. Perhaps you remember a concern that came to you during the prayer period and that you let go of. Now is the time to let it come back to you as a petition for others, for now it is arising as an expression of the prayer in secret. Because you let go of it during your practice period by returning to your sacred word, allowing the prayer and even your heartfelt concern for someone's suffering to be enfolded by the mystery of God, you can trust that it is now coming back through you as Christ's prayer. Align your own intention with Christ's prayers for the world.

You can also consciously integrate your sacred word and activity—the activity of your mind or external activity. For example, you can visualize yourself in the coming activity of the day and at the same time let your sacred word come to you. In this way, you are, in effect, blessing the activity with the giftedness of your sitting receptive practice, as your sacred word arises out of your prayer period into the imagined activity of your day.

As we practice deepening the sacred word in centering prayer, we consent to God's Sacred Word, Christ, which allows us to enter more fully into the Christian contemplative life—a life of greater freedom, joy, and meaning. The same attitudes and means can also deepen our use of the other sacred symbols—the sacred breath, the sacred glance, and the sacred nothingness—all of which deepen our experience of God.

CHAPTER FOUR

Deepening the Sacred Breath

God's breath it was that made me; the breathing of
Shaddai [God] that gave me life.

—Job 33:4[1]

As mentioned in the previous chapters, while the basic teaching on centering prayer generally focuses on the use of the sacred word, it is also possible to practice with other sacred symbols, including the sacred breath. Because the breath is such an embodied and receptive symbol, many people are drawn to practicing centering prayer with the sacred breath at certain seasons of the spiritual journey, to help with the deepening of their prayer into contemplation and as a way of integrating and embodying their spiritual practice with their physical, human experience.

God is the creator and sustainer of life. God's indwelling presence is the source of your life—your everyday existence and your interior awareness. In the Hebrew language of Jesus's time, the word that means "spirit" and "breath" is the same: *ruah*. John writes that after the resurrection, Jesus gave his followers the gift of ruah, transmitting the Spirit to his disciples through his own breath: "he breathed on them and said to them, 'Receive the Holy Spirit'" (John 20:22). The breath has long been a symbol for the Spirit of God, the Holy Spirit.

Because we are created in the image of God, our physical breath is a created, immanent image of the uncreated, transcendent breath of God. The Holy Spirit is the breath of God, the breath within our breath. The Spirit animates our life as our breath breathes in us, from the moment of birth until the instant of death: "Then the Lord God formed man from the dust of the ground, and breathed into his nostrils the breath of life; and the man became a living being" (Genesis 2:7). The Spirit of God, the experience that Christ gives to his followers as the animating force of their prayer, breathes in us, within everything we do in prayer and life.

We are usually not aware of the Spirit in us, just as we are usually not aware of our breath. Scripture invites us to greater awareness: "Don't you know that you yourselves are God's temple and that God's Spirit dwells in you?" (1 Corinthians 3:16). In centering prayer, your breath can symbolize your consent to God's presence and action. Because the breath is such a rich symbol of God's indwelling presence, practicing with the sacred breath opens you to greater awareness of the Spirit's presence and action in you and in all of life. Indeed, deepening the sacred breath in centering prayer transforms your awareness itself.

How do you practice with the sacred breath? In the basic teaching on centering prayer in *Open Mind, Open Heart,* Thomas Keating writes:

> Noticing one's breathing can also serve as a sacred symbol of one's consent to God's presence and action within. In this case, one does not follow one's breathing physically as is done in some Eastern forms of meditation, but simply observes it. In centering prayer the purpose is not simply to let go of all thoughts but to deepen our contact with the Divine Indwelling. The intentionality of faith is fundamental.[2]

This introductory instruction on how to practice with the breath touches on its richness as a sacred symbol in centering prayer. But that is all the basic teaching says about how to do it. This chapter describes how to deepen the sacred breath in centering prayer.

The Sacred Breath for Certain Seasons of the Spiritual Journey

As mentioned in the last chapter, the practice of centering prayer naturally deepens and unfolds across the seasons of the spiritual journey. The more contemplative focus of praying with the sacred word, which we explored in the previous chapter, builds upon the foundation of the basic guidelines of centering prayer. The active contemplative attitudes involved in deepening the sacred word are especially helpful during the season of the spiritual journey that John of the Cross calls the "active night of sense." Later, God relates to us more passively in what John calls the "passive night of sense."

In the passive night of sense, a receptive kind of purification begins in us. "To purify" means to cleanse, to eliminate, to make clean. The most important thing that is purified in contemplation is your sense of being separate from God. In centering prayer, you are cleansed of the inner obstacles to your union with Christ. You are wiped clean of your unawareness of the Spirit's presence in all things. The feeling that you are separate from God is an ongoing problem across many seasons of the journey and is especially acute during the passive night of sense. The Spirit—the Sacred Breath of God—purifies you of your felt separation from God.

To give an example, one woman who had been faithfully practicing centering prayer for about five years went through a period of emotional purification as she experienced a great deal of unresolved grief and anger about her husband's death. She felt that God was absent in her prayer because she was no longer experiencing joy and peacefulness during her practice. Even though her practice with the sacred word had become very receptive, she found that her sacred word kept her in her thinking mind, unconsciously resisting the Spirit's purification of her emotions. She was now in the passive night of sense, and when she tried practicing with the sacred breath, she discovered that it gave her a different ability—the ability to be with God amidst the sadness and anger. Grieving, mourning, letting go is a way into deeper life, into deeper relationship with God. Resisting and repressing feelings separates you from the healing presence and transforming action of the Spirit.

The sacred breath's embodied quality made this woman more aware of the felt sense of her body, more open to her feelings, and more able to experience her difficult emotions in God's presence. At this stage in her journey, using the sacred breath was the best way to practice the passivity or receptivity to God that John recommends during sense and emotional purification. The separate-self sense is purified when we are receptive to God in all things, including and especially emotions. The sacred breath is the most receptive symbol you can use in relating with God and is very helpful as the spiritual journey unfolds through its seasons, especially the passive ones.

Another person who benefited greatly from deepening the sacred breath was a longtime centering prayer practitioner in her late seventies who rarely used her sacred word in prayer any longer. After twenty-five years of daily practice, she found that God was relating to her more directly in contemplation, beyond any symbol or support. But she found that at times when she was plagued by strong emotions or obsessive thoughts, she still needed a symbol to return to, in order to renew and focus her consent to God. Emotional purification recurs at deeper levels on the spiritual journey, even for someone like this woman, who had already gone through the passive night of sense. Learning to renew her consent with her breath instead of the word was very liberating for this advanced centering prayer practitioner. She said that introducing the word was too hard, too harsh, for the way God was present for her. The breath was easy, natural, and ever-present, like the way God was now relating with her. She could effortlessly touch on her breath as a way of saying yes to God, and she could easily let it go to receive God's formless presence.

Deepening the sacred breath can be a valuable approach to centering prayer in any spiritual season. There are people who do well practicing with the sacred breath right from the beginning of the spiritual journey. When teaching centering prayer to college-age students, I find that many young adults connect with the breath because it is such an embodied symbol of consent to God. Young people are often physically active, may be drawn to embodied forms of contemplative practice such as hatha yoga or Buddhist mindfulness meditation, and are interested to learn that there is a tradition of embodied contemplative practice in Christianity. The younger generation sometimes finds that with the practice of the sacred word, a dualistic attitude develops between the body and the spirit, whereas with the sacred breath, there is no such split. The breath unites the body and spirit in prayer.

Say Yes to God's Indwelling Presence

In deepening the sacred breath in centering prayer, you simply notice the breath when you are engaged with thinking about other thoughts. In this way, you say yes to God's indwelling presence—a presence so close you are not normally aware of it because you are identified with your thoughts and emotions rather than with the divine life within.

The surface of your awareness is like the surface of a river that is filled with boats. You jump from boat to boat, living solely among the activity and noise of the surface. You know of nothing else. But when you discover the depths that lie beneath the surface of the river, you can dive down and be refreshed and freed from the activity and noise of the surface. The surface activity of the river is still there, but now you also know something deeper. By also knowing the depths, you are free from being defined only by surface noise and activity. You have a place to rest and be quiet.

Your thoughts are like those boats on the river, occupying you so that you never know the depths of God's indwelling presence. As you let go of thinking about thoughts, you open to God's ever-present depths. Practicing centering prayer, especially practicing with the sacred breath, helps you open to God's depths and dis-identify with your surface thoughts and emotions. Deepening the sacred breath opens you to God and, in particular, to what Teresa of Avila calls the "prayer of quiet."

The prayer of quiet sounds wonderful, doesn't it? It sounds as if your thoughts and thinking mind were always still and silent in prayer. Actually, Teresa describes this state of contemplative prayer as one in which your will is quiet while you can still experience distracting thoughts as your intellect roams around like a madman within you.[3] She makes the point that the prayer of quiet includes times when you are aware of the surface of your mind and the depths of awareness at the same time. The thoughts continue roaming around the surface of awareness like madmen, but when you quiet your will in the immediacy of God's presence in awareness, the mad thoughts are just surface noise. When you let go of fighting and resisting thoughts and consent to God by simply noticing your breath, you open to two levels of awareness at the same time. You can be aware of thoughts while at the same time resting in their source—an experience opened to you through awareness of your breath as the ever-present source of your life.

The prayer of quiet is very liberating because you begin to experience freedom amidst thoughts. Being free from thoughts, resting in the depths of the river away from the surface noise in interior silence, is indeed a valuable experience on the spiritual journey. But your relationship with God will be limited until you also learn how to be free in thoughts. If you are always searching for a transcendent peace free from thoughts, your spiritual life will not be fully integrated with the busyness and diversity of human life. Teresa of Avila says that the great benefits of the prayer of quiet are shown in daily life, as your will rests deeply in God while your other faculties of intellect and memory are free to engage actively in service.[4] You can even use the gift of human reflection in creative ways to help others while you are resting in God.

Practicing with the sacred breath is a wonderful way of learning and living the disposition that is at the heart of contemplation: amen, so be it. Deepening the sacred breath in centering prayer purifies or quiets not so much the madmen in your mind, but your struggle against the madmen in your mind. Sanity is when you stop going crazy about your own inner craziness. You learn detachment from thoughts, struggle, and the separate-self sense as the divine life acts more fully within you. Your will is quiet because it is learning to just be in God's presence in awareness, even while you are fully aware of the madmen in your mind. Practicing centering prayer with the sacred breath helps you relate to God amidst all thoughts, but especially amidst emotionally charged thoughts, the thoughts that resist what is going on and that you resist. With faithful, receptive practice of the sacred breath in centering prayer, you allow your will to be quiet, and you more easily let God's presence in awareness enfold and quiet the resistance and the emotionally charged thoughts that reinforce your sense of separation from the divine.

God's Presence in Pure Awareness

As the prayer of quiet deepens, attention and awareness are transformed. Attention is the focusing or directing of the human capacity to be aware. I can direct my will to and focus attention externally on any object of the world. I can also focus my will and attention internally on my thoughts, feelings, or body perceptions. Awareness is the ground in consciousness in which all internal and external objects exist, like the waters of a river upon which boats float. Awareness is different from any object of thought, feeling, or perception and different from the act of focusing attention on these objects.

One of the benefits of practicing centering prayer with the sacred breath is that your intention—the heart of centering prayer—is brought to life by a gentle movement of attentive consent: noticing your breath when you are engaged with thoughts. The attentive consent that brings intention to life is what makes deepening the sacred breath a more embodied way of practicing centering prayer than praying with the sacred word. Centering prayer is not a practice of attention alone, for you let go of even this gentle noticing of your breathing. Your consent comes to life as you rest in God; you let go of attention to your breath and just are, in God's presence in pure awareness. Thomas Keating calls this the "birth of spiritual attentiveness."[5] Because centering prayer is primarily a contemplative practice of intention and consent, attention is in skillful service of a greater yes to God's indwelling presence in pure awareness, not the symbol of the breath alone, not the act of focusing will or attention.

God's indwelling presence manifests in pure awareness, not any object of awareness. That is why contemplative teachers like John of the Cross are so concerned about not getting attached to any perception, thought, or spiritual entity. Likewise, in centering prayer the symbol you practice with is not God. The symbol merely represents your consent to God's presence and action within. In practicing with the sacred breath, you do not attend to your breathing continuously, for that would be focusing your will on an object that is just passing, not resting in God's eternal, timeless presence. But the breath can be an especially helpful symbol of consent to God because it is ever-present in awareness and easily attended to, rather than thought about. The breath is such a receptive symbol. It is easy to let go of the breath and just be, and as you do so, your prayer becomes more transparent to God's presence in pure awareness.

The difference between attention and awareness parallels the relationship between centering prayer, in which you begin practicing in relationship to a symbol, and contemplation, in which you just are, resting, being, in God. Thomas Keating says that in deep contemplation,

> the place to which we are going is one in which the knower, the knowing, and that which is known are all one. Awareness alone remains . . . [I]f you are not thinking, there is not even the thought that you are not thinking. There is just pure awareness, and that is the proximate goal of contemplative prayer.[6]

Deepening the sacred breath in centering prayer allows you to become one with God's indwelling presence in pure awareness. The one who is breathing, the breathing itself, and the breath are united in God. There is just God's presence acting in you, the breath of God breathing in you.

As Thomas Keating points out, there is still a dualistic separation when you are peacefully aware of God: you are the subject who is aware of God's peace. You are resting in the depths of the river, aware of but separate from the activity on the surface of the river. In deepening the sacred breath in centering prayer, when you are aware of thoughts, you notice your breathing. The breath becomes a receptive, open window through which you can more easily receive God. Yet in the deepening movements of this practice, you let go of the sacred breath itself and are just in God. Letting go of the breath and being in God's presence itself orients you toward pure awareness. With time, surrender, and the integration of prayer into service, moments of being in pure awareness develop over the spiritual journey to the point where your identity is rooted in union with God.

Thus, experiences of finding freedom from thoughts and freedom in thoughts are brought to a new level in you. When Christ's presence acts in your prayer, the gentle radiance of the Trinitarian life effortlessly awakens in pure awareness. You do not need to be the subject who is experiencing it or have any object to your experience. You realize the truth of Paul's scriptural statement, "It is no longer I who live, but it is Christ who lives in me" (Galatians 2:20). It is not you who lives; Christ lives in you. In union with God, you are not aware of God as an object outside of you because Christ is the subject inside of you, looking out through your eyes. There is nothing to be aware of, for you are in the radiance of pure awareness, the life of God as it manifests inside you. The separate-self sense is lost in the cloud of forgetting, in the immediacy of God. Pure awareness is the effect in consciousness of eternity breaking into time. In God's presence in pure awareness, there is no past or future. Life just is, in God.

Be Present to the Divine Presence

God is beyond our interior worlds and our psychological experiences, yet our interior worlds and psychological experiences are in God. In Jesus's parables of the kingdom of God—a realm that is not found in things that can be observed—he said that life is not found by searching or struggling but is discovered within you or among you (Luke 17:20–21).

In deepening contemplation, you realize the living gift of the indwelling presence of God, beyond and within and around your thoughts, emotions, efforts, and struggles. God's indwelling presence in awareness enfolds and holds and infuses everything—all thoughts, all struggle, all striving—without judgment or exclusion, without resistance or attachment. At the deepest level of union with the divine presence flows action, service to others that is freer of self. This service may not be big, showy, or even noticeable. This form of service may be hidden, unseen, but very real to anyone whose perception is refined enough to appreciate it—just like God.

The Receptive Contemplative Attitudes with the Sacred Breath

Part II of this book will look in depth at eight receptive contemplative attitudes: giving God your consent to act in you, recognizing God, awakening in God, effortlessness, letting be, being, being embraced in Christ, and emerging in prayer and life. In order to describe more fully how to deepen the sacred breath in centering prayer, each of the eight following sections applies one of the eight attitudes to the sacred breath. With time, these receptive attitudes commingle with your active dispositions, and your contemplative practice becomes more integrated.

The actual practice of deepening the sacred breath in centering prayer is very simple. Everything you learn in centering prayer's basic guidelines remains the foundation of your contemplative practice. You just allow a very receptive relationship to unfold with your symbol, your breath. When engaged with your thoughts, notice your breathing, effortlessly in you, like God.

Recognizing God with the Sacred Breath

Recognize that the gift of God's indwelling presence, given to you through Christ, is closer to you than you are to yourself—closer than your breathing, closer than consciousness itself. Your breath is a symbol of the closeness, the intimacy of God. Your breath, like God, is always with you in this life, from the moment of your birth until the instant of your death.

God is the ground of life itself. God's Being is intertwined with human being. Of course, you do not always feel God's presence, especially during suffering. Contemplative practice, faith, and prayer penetrate the mystery of God's felt absence in suffering, evil, purification, and spiritual darkness by allowing your consciousness to settle beneath or within these experiences into a deeper truth. Deepening the sacred breath in centering prayer enables you to settle into God's subtle indwelling presence and live more from that presence.

Notice how your breath actually works in you. You don't have to find it, really. There is no need to search for it. Your breath is there in you, always, just like God. You are not normally aware of it because your awareness is caught on the surface of your being, identified with thoughts, emotions, and concerns. However, see what it is like to just recognize your breath in you. Simply notice it, already existing in you. Your breath is already in you the way God is already in you. Simply recognize it, as a very receptive practice of faith that trusts in the grace, the giftedness of God. You are aware of your breath, and your awareness quiets into the moment. Thoughts and feelings may still roam around like madmen on the surface of your awareness, but you recognize your breath again and again. Recognizing God is the first receptive attitude, an attitude that easily comes to life as you deepen the sacred breath in centering prayer.

Giving God Your Consent to Act in You through the Sacred Breath

Taking a moment to prepare your body is especially important for deepening the sacred breath in centering prayer. Having a natural, alert, open, and receptive physical posture expresses the inner posture of the practice. In deepening the sacred breath, your eyes can be closed or open. Normally, closing your eyes in centering prayer gives you a little more focus, as you let go of visual images from the world around you. Yet you may find that keeping your eyes open and unfocused while gently resting your gaze in front of you also helps your prayer to deepen. But instead of following your thoughts about what you see, notice your breath while your eyes are open and seeing. Keeping your eyes open can actually balance your practice amidst intense thoughts or physical tiredness. Because the breath is such an embodied symbol of consenting to God, having your eyes open to the world around you opens you to the Creator of everything, the presence acting in you and in everything that exists.

As you prepare yourself—your body and your intention—for the formal period of centering prayer, renew your consent to God's indwelling presence by observing your breath, beyond and beneath and within your thoughts. Like God, your breath is a presence that acts, that breathes, in you. Notice your breath, present and moving in you, as a symbol of the way God's presence lives and acts in you. Observing your breath is a way of opening yourself to God, a way of responding to the gift of life.

Awakening to God through the Sacred Breath

In deepening the sacred breath in centering prayer, your practice is very simple: when engaged with your thoughts, notice your breathing, effortlessly in you, like God. Noticing your breathing is a very receptive movement of faith. Faith in the context of contemplation is a gift beyond concepts, images, and thoughts. As waking up from a dream frees you from illusion, faith breaks you open to new life with God.

God's presence is always available to you. But too often your thoughts, the activity of thinking about your thoughts, and the sense of self as a separate subject behind thoughts and thinking distract you from the life of faith and God's presence. All you have to do is receive God, awaken to the gift of God's presence, already given to you. The breath is a wonderful symbol that helps you receive God, in faith, because your breath is always with you in some way or other. Just notice your breathing—shallow or heavy, in your belly or in your chest—when you are engaged with another thought, as a way of consenting to God's unseen, unknown life within. Practicing all the other contemplative attitudes with the sacred breath expands on this basic attitude of receptive faith.

Effortlessness with the Sacred Breath

Your breathing happens in you without you having to make it happen. Your breathing, God's presence, and contemplation itself are gifts that you don't have to find. In contemplation you are found in God, more and more at one with God's presence and action. Of course, practicing with the sacred breath, you become more aware of your breathing, which may include becoming more self-aware, more self-conscious. You may become engaged with thoughts about your body, thinking about how you are breathing, thinking about trying to breathe, or thinking about settling your breath. That's fine. Just return to your breathing as a way of consenting to God. Let your return to your breath be as effortless as the way your breath breathes in you. Let your breath pray in you, effortlessly, like the Spirit.

Becoming more aware of your interior life is not a problem in contemplative practice, although it may feel like it at times. You have to go through greater self-awareness in order to become more aware of God. You have to go through greater self-awareness in order to let God awaken you to pure awareness. Just notice your breathing. Let your breathing regain its effortless quality in you, like God's effortlessness in you. As you attune yourself to God's effortlessness through noticing your breathing, you too will become more effortless. It is your practice of returning to your breath that allows the Spirit to pray in you, without you trying to make it happen. The Spirit enfolds your self-consciousness; your self-awareness, as your will, your effort, releases on its own.

Letting Be in the Sacred Breath

God cannot be controlled in prayer. Deepening the sacred breath in centering prayer is a wonderful way of learning how to relate to God, for this way of prayer has nothing to do with controlling your breathing. Rather, you just return your attention to the way your breath is in you. There is a sense in which your breath settles with this practice, from your chest to your belly, but it does so as a by-product of your receptivity, of your letting go of trying to breathe in any special way. Your breath settles because you are saying yes to God. The relationship with God settles everything.

A better way of describing this aspect of the practice is that you return to your breathing instead of your breath. Returning to your *breath* is returning to a noun, a thing. Returning to your *breathing* is returning to a verb—a living, dynamic action—which is the way God is present in you. So to return to the way your breathing is in you is to return to the way God is in you—dynamic, changing, beyond your control. The Spirit is a living, transforming presence acting in you. Align your prayer with the Spirit's action in you by just returning your attention to the way your breathing is in you.

Being in the Sacred Breath of God

Let go of returning to your breath and just be—be in open, receptive awareness of God's mystery. As with all ways to deepen the practice of centering prayer with the sacred symbols, the contemplative attitude of *being* is about letting go of the symbol itself to move into God's mystery that is beyond form and symbol. You let go of returning to your breath, let your breath just be, and let yourself just be, in God's presence in awareness and beyond awareness. Scripture says, "God's breath it was that made me; the breathing of Shaddai [God] that gave me life" (Job 33:4).[7] In order to let centering prayer deepen into contemplation, let go of noticing your physical breath, so that God's breath breathes itself in you. The life that you are given by God, the life you are given by God's breathing, is beyond symbols, concepts, and anything that is normally called psychological. God's presence is more ontological—rooted in the nature of being itself. So letting go of noticing your breathing brings you into deep receptivity, into the fullness of contemplation itself. Then you can see how the physical and the psychological—indeed, how everything—is an expression, a creation of the mystery of God, the source of all life.

Being Embraced in Christ

You may notice strong feelings. Become one with your breathing as you attend to the feelings; let feelings just be in your awareness. Continually return to your breath and let the Spirit enfold and embrace strong feelings with you. This attitude is very important for responding to the emotional purification that comes, and returns, on the contemplative journey. Emotional purification brings you to greater freedom, yet purification recurs on deeper levels.

This is where your understanding of the deepening practice of centering prayer helps. Let's talk about the deepening of centering prayer on the two levels of practice we've explored so far: deepening the sacred word and deepening the sacred breath. Remember that you learned how to let go of returning to your sacred word and embrace feelings as your symbol of consent to God's presence and action. Remember how you embrace God in the feeling. As you open to God, your relationship with the feeling changes. The afflictive emotion is found in God. This is the ground you need to establish in order to be embraced by God during the more encompassing emotional purification that comes with the passive phase of the dark night of sense.

In deepening the sacred breath, you go further in learning to respond to the more profound way God is coming to life, consciously, in you, for behind the emotional purification that you are called upon to actively embrace is a more profound emptiness. In practicing centering prayer with the sacred breath, you learn how to be embraced by Christ in situations like passive purification. The sacred breath, because it is such an embodied symbol, is what helps you. You let yourself become one with your breath in the emptiness, relaxing into it, and find God in the emptiness behind the emotion. Discovering that God is in the emptiness is what transforms the separate-self sense. Remember, God's presence in awareness is coming alive to you as you practice with the sacred breath. The separate-self sense is enfolded, held, and gently released by God through the mediation of your consent within the sacred breath. You do not escape emotional pain by practicing centering prayer. Rather, by deepening the sacred breath in centering prayer you are able to be present in pain through Christ's indwelling presence. God's presence embraces you in the pain. Become one with this embrace; simply experience the pain while you are returning to your breath, and then, in a further movement, allow yourself to be held by God's presence in awareness.

Your training—your actions and your receptivity—come together, embracing God in the emotion and being embraced by Christ in the emptiness behind emotions. The separate-self sense lets go more easily, and your identity in God comes to life more consciously. There is no need to feel overwhelmed by or concerned about what to do. Remember, the approach described in this book is based on cooperating with God as you gradually experience the divine life coming to life in you. Embracing and being embraced are attitudes that help this process unfold. Emotional reactivity, resistance, and emptiness are the problems, the obstacles that are released and purified when your contemplative practice becomes a little more skillful, a little more attuned to God.

Emerging in Prayer and Life on the Breath of God

As in the basic guidelines of centering prayer and in practicing centering prayer with the sacred word, you allow a transitional period between your sitting in practice and your activity, allowing the fruits of prayer to blossom in your life. There are many ways of bridging the sitting practice of centering prayer with the rest of your activities. One way to do this with the sacred breath is to simply visualize or think about some activity while noticing your breathing; in this way, you intentionally bless your day's activities with the same consent that you have had during your silent prayer period.

God's presence in awareness is like the cinema screen upon which all of a film's images are projected. At the movies, we normally are quite caught up in its drama and not aware of the screen. At the end of the movie, if we stay long enough, we will finally see the screen that was there all along, silently, secretly holding the film. Similarly, at the end of your own movie, your own life's story, you will experience the reality that silently, secretly held you throughout your whole life: God's presence. Why not realize this presence during life? Then, you can be aware of God at the same time as you live your ordinary life. You can be at one with the screen and the movie at the same time.

CHAPTER FIVE

Deepening the Sacred Glance

*You have died, and your life is hidden with Christ in
God. When Christ who is your life is revealed, then you
also will be revealed with him in glory.*

—Colossians 3:3–4

Before we explore how to practice centering prayer with the
sacred glance, let's take a moment and recall the context for
the teachings in this book. The best way to support contemplative
practice is not by dispensing information in a pedantic manner,
trying to provide help from the outside in. Real spiritual growth
is initiated within you; it happens from the inside out. In contemplative learning, the right insight is joined with your own inner
wisdom, the obstacles and the resistances to the divine life within
you lessen, and a seed is planted that helps your practice unfold.
This book is not meant to pile information on you or confuse you
about what to do in prayer. The chapters on deepening the sacred
symbols in centering prayer are not meant to change what you
are doing. Rather, they offer seeds for your practice. Not all of
these seeds will take root, but with the right inner receptivity, a

few—the ones that are right for you—will grow over time in you. As we explore another aspect of the deepening practice of centering prayer, the sacred glance, listen with your heart and let the Spirit within be evoked in that listening.

The Basic Instruction on the Sacred Glance

Thomas Keating briefly describes how to practice centering prayer with the third sacred symbol, the sacred glance: "If you find that a visual symbol is more helpful, use it, provided, of course, that you introduce it silently and return to it whenever you notice you are engaged with some other thought. A visual symbol should be general, not clear and precise."[1] Notice that he does not say to concentrate on an image, to let your imagination unfold in a dreamlike state, or to generate a concrete, detailed visualization. He does not say to rest your gaze on an icon to receive the symbolic blessings contained within it. Those are different forms of contemplative practice.

The way Thomas Keating speaks about the sacred glance in centering prayer is the same way he speaks of the sacred word. The content of the image, like the content of the sacred word, is not as important as the way you return to it as a symbol of your consent to the presence and action of God. When practicing with the sacred glance, you may use an image, but you don't concentrate on it.

The image associated with the sacred glance can be of Christ, but the image does not need to be overtly religious. You might turn inward toward a color, light, or just an inner spaciousness. Just as you choose one sacred word and let that single word become identified with your consent to God over time rather than changing your word from prayer period to prayer period, you practice the sacred glance with the same image over time. When you practice with the sacred breath, you are simply noticing your breathing rather than directing your breathing in some particular way. Similarly, with the sacred glance you ever so gently turn and return to your image when engaged with your thoughts. This returning is not about creating a detailed visualization that you hold in your mind.

In the early years of centering prayer, we used the term *sacred gaze* for this symbol. But experience showed that the term *sacred glance* evoked less effort in people drawn to this way of practicing centering prayer. Imagine you are sitting by the sea, sharing an incredible view with your beloved, and you become distracted by the conversation of the couple next to you. The talk you hear nearby doesn't have to affect your own relationship. All you need to do is silently turn toward your partner to renew your sense of connection. There is no need to stare at your partner, for in doing so you will lose what you are really sharing, which is the vast beauty before you. Likewise, in centering prayer you are really relating to the vast spaciousness of God, beyond image and form. Each of the sacred symbols, including the sacred glance, helps you remain present to an unseen and unseeable mystery. If you concentrate on an image, if you gaze steadily at it rather than ever so gently returning to it, you may miss the spacious beauty of God.

Contemplative prayer is like being in a dark room, knowing that another person is present with you, but because of the absence of light, you are unable to see them. You practice by turning toward them in the darkness. The turning, the glancing, is not meant to penetrate or illuminate the darkness, but rather to consent to the presence of the other hidden within the darkness. In line with the teaching of *The Cloud of Unknowing,* deepening the sacred glance in centering prayer is a contemplative practice of "unknowing" to the intellectual mind. The unknowing means not trying to see God clearly through the sacred symbol.

Thomas Keating uses another metaphor to bring forth the nuances of the sacred glance: "Some people find it especially helpful to pray before the Blessed Sacrament. They usually keep their eyes closed and are simply aware of the presence in which they are praying."[2] When engaged with your thoughts, you just turn inwardly toward the presence you trust is there, without needing to open your eyes to see it. To deepen the sacred glance in centering prayer, when engaged with your thoughts, ever so gently turn to God's unseen presence within. Deepening the sacred glance in centering prayer is that simple. The most important aspect of practicing centering prayer with the sacred glance is the visual turning and returning that is consenting to the presence and action of God. As contemplation unfolds in you, God's presence becomes less dualistic, more unseeable, and more real.

Your Unique Spiritual Learning Style

Now that the general approach to centering prayer with the sacred glance has been described, let's look at who might benefit by practicing in this way. Sometimes when I work with people who have already established their daily practice of centering prayer, I explore with them how the psycho-spiritual theory of learning styles might affect their spiritual practice. Psychological research has shown that humans have different, unique styles for processing information based on the different senses.[3]

Consider the three main senses: sound, sense, and sight. According to the theory of learning styles, people can be distinguished by which of these three sense channels they learn best through. For example, the auditory learner processes information from the outer world primarily through sound (auditorily) and secondarily through sense (kinesthetically) or sight (visually). At a lecture, the auditory learner will tune into the speaker's words more than the PowerPoint images. The visual learner naturally uses sight and greatly benefits from seeing the lecturer and images. This person also learns better when the teacher uses imagery when speaking. The kinesthetic learner takes in information in a more bodily way, accessing sensation, movement, and feeling. At a lecture, this person does best by "feeling" into the topic. This person thinks conceptually, yet has a keen "felt sense" when thinking and perceiving. As children in school, kinesthetic learners need to move about in their chairs, not necessarily because they are not paying attention, but because physical movement helps them to learn. The physical movement seems to correspond to some kind of movement of the mind, helping them to process and assimilate information better. Identifying your primary sense channel can be very helpful in communication, in understanding others, and even in spiritual practice. Consider for a moment which is your primary learning style: auditory, visual, or kinesthetic.

Thomas Keating's teaching on centering prayer skillfully offers three types of sacred symbols: the word, the breath, and the glance. The sacred word is often a more natural way of practicing centering prayer for auditory learners. Returning ever so gently to the sound of the sacred word when engaged with your thoughts can naturally help you hear the word pray itself within you and then help you let go of the form of the word into interior silence. The sacred breath is often a more helpful symbol for kinesthetic learners. Noticing the felt sense of your breathing when engaged with your thoughts can naturally help you effortlessly yield to the Spirit and then let go of the breath to experience inner stillness. The sacred glance is often a more helpful symbol for visual learners. Ever so gently turning to a visual image within you when engaged with your thoughts can naturally help you open into the unseeable mystery of God and then let go of the glance to experience inner spaciousness.

As these brief descriptions reinforce, the point of centering prayer is not to hang onto your sacred symbol, but to return to it as a way of consenting to God's living mystery beyond form or symbol. In contemplative practice, you are not processing information, but allowing the sacred symbol to move beyond conscious form into God.

The sacred nothingness, the fourth sacred symbol, which will be explored in the following chapters, is the most contemplative way of practicing centering prayer. If you are drawn to practicing centering prayer with the sacred nothingness, you may also find that your learning style affects the primary way you experience the presence of God as "no thing," beyond form or symbol. Interior silence is often the primary formless way of apprehending God for auditory learners. Interior stillness is often the primary formless way of apprehending God for kinesthetic learners. Interior spaciousness is often the primary formless way of apprehending God for visual learners. Once you recognize your primary way of apprehending God, the others can radiate within you, in God. Silence, stillness, and spaciousness dance as the Trinity awakens in its nothingness— the source of everything. Which sense metaphor is most descriptive of your contemplative experience: silence, stillness, or spaciousness?

In the context of centering prayer, knowing your style of learning can be helpful, but it is only a relative tool. There are many factors, including grace, involved in the choice and use of your sacred symbol. This theory is not meant to complicate your established way of prayer. I find great diversity in people's experience of the sacred symbols. For example, one practitioner who used a sacred word in his centering prayer didn't change his symbol when he discovered he was primarily a kinesthetic learner. Instead, he recognized the ways he was *feeling* or *sensing* his sacred word returning to him as his prayer deepened. Recognizing this movement helped him continue and deepen his practice with the sacred word.

This psycho-spiritual theory on learning styles was not used when centering prayer was first being taught in the 1970s. Rather, centering prayer is based upon hundreds of years of lived experience.

Over these centuries, communities of contemplatives articulated more skillful ways of practicing, based on their needs, understanding, and experiences, just as people have done with centering prayer in the last decades. The theory of learning styles can shed wonderful insight on the benefits of the sacred symbols. Spiritual direction with a director experienced in contemplation and centering prayer is often the best way of applying this theory to your practice. However, for the purposes of this introduction to deepening the sacred glance in centering prayer, if you are a visual learner, you might consider the benefits of using this symbol in your practice.

The Image of God in the Purification Process

As we have seen, the content or meaning of the sacred symbol is not as important as the way you practice with it. This is true of both the sacred word and the sacred glance. However, as some people choose a sacred word that represents who God is for them, if you are practicing with the sacred glance, you can use an image whose meaning helps to deepen your prayer. As explored in Chapter 2, you can foster intention prior to beginning centering prayer by remembering who God is for you, now. The meaning of the sacred symbol can express this sense of who God is for you. Remember, once the period of centering prayer begins, you don't reflect on the meaning of your word or your image. Rather, your practice of centering prayer brings the meaning of your symbol to a new level—the transformation, in Christ, of your mind, awareness, heart, and being—*because* you don't reflect on the meaning of the symbol.

In spiritual direction, I once gave a longtime practitioner of centering prayer an image for her practice with the sacred glance, and it helped get her through an intense period of purification. This woman had lost the sense of her relationship with Christ. Christ's love had always been a wonderful support for her spiritual journey. She had a keen appreciation of his presence, which was mediated to her through the gift of his sacrificial love. But now she felt that Christ had abandoned her. She was experiencing feelings of despair and self-judgment that made it very hard for her to continue her practice. As we explored her symptoms, especially the subtle energies of the unconscious that became evident within her feelings and thoughts, I saw that she was in the season of the spiritual journey that John of the Cross calls "the dark night of spirit."

To help this woman work through this period of purification, I suggested that in centering prayer she could practice with the sacred glance toward an image of Christ's Anastasis. *Anastasis* in Greek means the "harrowing of hell" and is a profound, though not well understood, aspect of the full revelation of the mystery of Christ. After the crucifixion, Christ descended into hell to free those souls trapped there by demons before his resurrection. The crucifixion is commemorated on Good Friday, the Anastasis is memorialized on Holy Saturday, and the Resurrection is celebrated on Easter Sunday. In icons, the mystery of the Anastasis is often depicted with Jesus underground in hell, blessing and freeing a multitude of souls, as demons hide in the background. Relying on the deepening mysteries of Christ's revelation can liberate you from the hellish realms of spiritual suffering, including suffering during centering prayer as it arises during the dark night of spirit.

How did the woman use this image in her practice? According to the basic guidelines of the sacred glance described earlier in this chapter, she did not look at or concentrate on an image of the Anastasis, did not reflect on it or supplicate it. Rather, the image of Christ's Anastasis was the sacred symbol she turned toward with an inward glance when she was engaged with any thought, including and especially thoughts about loss, temptation, despair, doubt, and the contraction into self that are so painful during the dark night of spirit.

After some time practicing centering prayer in this way, this woman moved through this difficult period. What was helpful about the image she used in her practice of centering prayer with the sacred glance? First, she learned that although she had lost the sense of her relationship with Jesus, she was, in fact, immersed in a new, important facet of the mystery of Christ. In a real way, the choice to use the Anastasis in her practice was not something that came from her imagination, one option chosen from many different images. The Anastasis—the harrowing of hell—was the spiritual reality that was going on in her. Recognizing this reality was the first step in making the grace within the Anastasis conscious and available to her in her practice. She was being led deeper by Christ into his transforming mystery: from Good Friday's crucifixion through Holy Saturday's harrowing of hell toward the resurrection of Easter Sunday. The dark night of spirit is about moving through the loss of God and of your own sense of self, about transforming destructive energies while stabilizing your contemplative practice in the subtle light of Christ's resurrected presence. Understanding how the mystery of Christ is available to you in your contemplative practice helps you negotiate the seasons of the spiritual journey more skillfully.

Second, she recognized the deep destructive energies that were arising in her thoughts and emotions and disrupting her life and practice, allowing guilt, shame, and despair to come into her consciousness in symbolic form as demons. In her centering prayer practice, she had a symbol of consent that visually represented the grace of God transforming these destructive energies. In the Anastasis icon, the demons are depicted symbolically in *relationship with Christ* and are transformed by this relationship. The Anastasis is the sacred mystery that brings the grace of Christ to deep destructive energies.

Third, the image expressed her trust that God is greater than the destructive energies. The image represented the woman's intention to turn more deeply toward God, an intention she cultivated prior to centering prayer. Through the sacred glance toward the image, she related to Christ's transformation of the demons, rather than trying to fight the demons on her own. As she began centering prayer, glancing toward the imagistic symbol but not holding onto it, she let the conscious intention become transformed into consent to God's presence and transforming action in her. By inwardly glancing toward the image when engaged with self-reflective thoughts, she allowed it to be sacred for her prayer. Thus, she was practicing according to the foundational principles of centering prayer.

What came next for this woman? Her trust in God, constant prayer, and determination to persevere in the spiritual journey—the three dispositions helpful during every time of temptation[4]—gradually opened her into the mystery of Christ's resurrection. As her prayer became more rooted in the Heart of God—Christ's living, resurrected presence as her own true self—the destructive energies that had been tormenting her became simple thoughts and feelings that were released, like any other thought or feeling, within her. Those who have gone through the dark night of spirit know that emotional purification often coexists with spiritual purification. Spirit and sense purification overlap. Because destructive energies arise in the imagination, the spiritual purification can be skillfully transformed through visual symbols and the sacred glance. Because the emotional purification arises in sensate experience, letting go of the sacred symbol and embracing God in the strong feelings is the skillful response in centering prayer. Both sides to the deepening practice of centering prayer involve consent, as God's presence and action come to full life in you.

The committed practice of centering prayer orients you toward the fullness of Christ's revelation that is beyond any destructive, demon-like energy. Your consent to God's presence and action at the ground of being is more profound than any emotion, image, or destructive energy that passes through consciousness. Some of these dynamics are best explored in spiritual direction, but having a more nuanced and skillful way of practicing centering prayer available to you can be very helpful during the dark nights. With understanding and skillful practice, the darkness, challenges, and storms are enfolded as a natural part of the seasons of the spiritual journey.

Forsaking Love for Love's Sake

Another example of how deepening the sacred glance helps with centering prayer also comes from spiritual direction. Once, I was working with a woman who was taking on new responsibilities as a presenter of introductory workshops on centering prayer. She had come to spiritual direction to discern with me, as she said, "if this was God's idea or my idea." This question is a good prerequisite for entering into any form of contemplative service, and I was glad she wanted to explore it.

In our first session, this woman described her rich mystical life and many experiences of God. We carefully considered her motivation for being a presenter on centering prayer, and at the end of the session, she chose to take on this new responsibility. Our next session came a month later, after she had given her first workshop. When she spoke about what happened the first time she taught, we both noticed a slight echo of self-satisfaction in her voice. Her description of the successful workshop included gratitude to God and healthy confidence in her abilities as a speaker about centering prayer, but she also spoke a lot about how teaching the event reflected upon her. A telling example came when she described some irritation she felt at her co-presenter. The way she spoke about this man's "lack of sophistication" made us both wonder whether her real concern was how she herself looked working alongside him, rather than whether the participants had received what they needed for learning centering prayer.

In spiritual direction, we explored how being more detached about her role could root her service in God. In the ensuing month, she began to pray before, during, and after the workshops. She also learned how to attend better to her thoughts about working with others. She renewed her sense of how to embrace God in her emotional reactions, and she formulated for her daily practice an intention that her service be transparent to God. But our examination of her centering prayer practice seemed to help her the most.

I asked her what was happening in her centering prayer. She said, "I see God and feel God's love continually during the centering prayer period. I use God's image as my sacred glance, and it helps me feel love. I think I am doing well in my prayer life. What is more important than feeling God's love?"

We talked about and affirmed the great gift of God's love. However, in her description of her experience, I also heard that she was focused on her spiritual experiences. I wondered how much her exterior attachment to her role as a presenter was tied to her interior attachment to her spiritual experiences. So for the rest of the session and over the course of the next few monthly meetings, the two of us explored together how refining her centering prayer practice could open her to a deeper relationship with God, the source of her feelings of love, and how this refinement could help her in her budding service as a presenter of centering prayer. I was grateful again for her honesty and commitment to deepening her prayer life, for as she renewed her understanding and practice, letting go of seeking the feeling of love in prayer, her service as a centering prayer presenter became more rooted in love.

This woman discovered, through her refined understanding and practice of centering prayer, that an image or even the felt sense of God's love is secondary to transformation in Christ. The contemplative teacher Cynthia Bourgeault shows how the core gesture of Jesus's life was self-emptying love, called *kenosis* in Greek.[5] Every meditation period involves participating in the emptying of self, in Jesus's kenosis.[6] In deepening the sacred glance in centering prayer, reflecting on the felt sense of love is the invitation to turn into the unknown, unknowable, and unseen presence of God within. There is a genuine self-emptying, or kenosis, in this kind of surrender when you "forsake love for love's sake," in the words of Hadewijch of Antwerp, the great Beguine contemplative of the thirteenth century.[7] For a contemplative, devoted to Christ and to his love, forsaking love for love's sake is a deep self-sacrifice, a deep letting go of that which feels like the most important thing in life.

In centering prayer, all the sacred symbols engender this kenotic, self-emptying love, but for some centering prayer practitioners, the sacred glance is especially helpful in this way. Many people with rich mystical lives also have rich lives of imagination. If these imaginative people practice centering prayer with the sacred glance, they are often prone to infusing an image with symbology from their own imagination or becoming attached to the image itself. In kenosis, God is always drawing you to detach from the sacred symbol. Some sacred symbols evoke your attachments and invite you to find a freer relationship with God. Spiritual direction with an experienced contemplative teacher and practitioner can help you as you enter into these subtle movements. If you are attached to your sacred symbol, you can choose a new one or learn to let go of its content. God is always bringing you into a more subtle relationship, which is engendered by a freer relationship with your symbol in centering prayer. As you progress, you learn how to receive this symbol from God and let it go back into God.

This is what the woman who was learning how to be a presenter on centering prayer discovered. As she became more detached from the content of her image and clung less to spiritual experiences, her service as a presenter of centering prayer also became freer. Detachment and freedom are the fruits of deepening centering prayer, whatever symbol you are using. Freedom manifests in life and in service, from the inside out, as a fruit of prayer.

Imagine a mirror that, amazingly, is polished over time into a clear window. The polishing clears away the image in the mirror that interferes with your clear vision. There is a similar transformation that comes with centering prayer. Attachment to roles and to spiritual experiences is a reflection of the separate-self sense and hinders your transparency to God. Deepening the sacred glance in centering prayer replaces your artificial self-image with God's living image. But this happens not through seeing God clearly, not by holding onto an image that reinforces the dualistic mind. Rather, the image of God comes to life within when you let go of trying to see God as a fixed object of mind. In scripture Paul speaks of the transformation of spiritual vision initiated through contemplative practice: "Now we see through a mirror, dimly, but then we will see face to face. Now I know only in part; then I will know fully, even as I have been fully known" (1 Corinthians 13:12). As we shall see, in practicing centering prayer with the sacred nothingness, the only way to "see" God face to face is to remain in the darkness of unknowing, where the dualistic way of perceiving, relating, and being is undone in you and *you become fully known.* Deepening the sacred glance in centering prayer is all about contemplative unknowing. When engaged with your thoughts, ever so gently turn to God's unseen presence within.

From Seeing to Being Seen by God

Whatever symbol you use in centering prayer, whatever practices you follow on your spiritual journey, as you let go of seeing clearly with the dualistic mind, you enter into a kind of union with God that is not based upon any one particular experience, even of Christ's love. The attitude of letting go transforms your self-will into willingness. The attitude of letting be invites an even deeper transformation as your will is united with God's will. The transformation of your mind, awareness, and heart is felt not so much as a single spiritual experience but as the ability to witness, or be aware of, all experiences without identifying with any of them. You don't identify with any one experience because, in deep letting go, your will and your sense of self are in union with God. That is why centering prayer is not focused on any one spiritual experience, but on letting all experiences go and on letting all experiences be without even trying to let them go.

In the traditional psychological understanding of Christian mystical theology, when the imagination and memory are united with God *along with the will* and its efforts to seek or hold onto spiritual experiences, you enter into a stage of contemplative prayer called the prayer of union. Thomas Keating says:

> God, so to speak, opens his heart to us and, to make sure that we don't miss the point or fail to receive the fullness of God's grace, puts to rest the mental obstacles in us by suspending the reflective faculties for a few moments or longer. . . . This is the Prayer of Union in which the will is completely united with God and one is fully aware of it.[8]

In contemplation you participate in the life of God. This includes participating in kenosis, Christ's self-emptying. The discipline of centering prayer is self-emptying, self-sacrificing, letting go of the limited sense of self that is separate from God, others, and all life. There are many ways to let go in centering prayer, but you can do it especially by (1) letting go of engaging with all thoughts, (2) letting go of the sacred symbol, and (3) letting go of spiritual experiences. By the disciplined letting go of all these objects of the mind, these *things,* you empty the experience of seeing God into a greater experience of being seen and known.

There is nothing wrong with thoughts, images, symbols, or spiritual experiences. The problem is with the separate-self sense that is conditioned by thoughts, images, symbols, and spiritual experiences. As you let go of trying to know God, trying to see God, you self-empty and are known and seen by God. As you let go of all self-effort to find God, a union is formed between your will and God's will. The spiritual witness, your sense of self as a subject of experience united with God in you, is a deeper identity than any role externally conditioned or tied to singular spiritual experiences.

Whatever sacred symbol you practice with in centering prayer, a deep kenosis, a profound self-emptying, is required. Deepening the sacred glance in centering prayer is a practice that is easily done if you are drawn to it by circumstances, by temperament, or in response to challenges in the unfolding seasons of your spiritual journey. Whether the sacred glance becomes your symbol in centering prayer or you use another symbol, the important thing is fidelity to the mystery of God. By whatever means, enter into union with Christ through your surrender and by the surrender of your surrender. Love God with your whole heart and strength and mind, and be loved by God as your heart, strength, and mind become one with God's. In this dying of self, you enter into union with God. You do not experience this union with your dualistic mind; you enter into it with the heart of your hearts. "You have died, and your life is hidden with Christ in God," Paul wrote in his letter to the Colossians (3:3–4). "When Christ who is your life is revealed, then you also will be revealed with him in glory."

CHAPTER SIX

Nothing but God's Silence, Stillness, and Spaciousness

*No eye has seen, no ear has heard, no mind has conceived
what God has prepared for those who love Him.*

—1 Corinthians 2:9

Now that we've explored how the three sacred symbols of word, breath, and glance build upon the foundation of the basic guidelines of centering prayer, let's explore the heart of Christian prayer itself, pure contemplation. As we continue on the spiritual journey, the experience of just resting and simply being in God without any symbol defines our prayer more and more. This is what is meant by pure contemplation. It is pure because it doesn't rely on anything to support its practice except God's formless, infinite mystery.

God can draw you beyond words, thoughts, sacred symbols, and your own actions at any time in your meditation. Whether you are practicing centering prayer with one of the sacred symbols or with no symbol, it is essential to learn to let go of words, thoughts, symbols, and effort and just rest, simply being in God. The contemplative attitudes we will explore in Part II, especially the receptive ones, point toward this subtle contemplative movement of resting, being in God without any words, thoughts, or symbols.

While pure contemplation is a gift rather than something that you do, there is a way in which the longtime practitioner learns what *not* to do. By learning how to practice centering prayer without relying on a symbol, you draw closer to this not doing. There is no symbol that you can use in pure contemplation, no thing that can represent your consent to God. Centering prayer in the light of pure contemplation is practiced with no symbol and can also be referred to as practicing with the sacred nothingness. Pure contemplation sheds light on how to practice centering prayer with the sacred nothingness; practicing centering prayer with no symbol helps you more easily receive the gift of pure contemplation. Of the four ways of deepening centering prayer described in this book, centering prayer with the sacred nothingness is the approach most suited to longterm practitioners. Yet beginners can benefit from learning about it because it will help them understand how their beginning practice, which normally requires a sacred symbol, matures over time as the path of centering prayer and their experience of God deepen.

Pray with No Thing

The great desert father and patriarch of Christian monasticism Anthony of the Desert said, "The prayer of the monk is not perfect until he no longer realizes himself or the fact that he is praying."[1] For monastic and nonmonastic contemplative practitioners alike, not to realize that you are praying means that you let go of thinking about how to pray. You let go of self-reflecting about what you are doing. You do not rely on a thought or concept or image of God. You are not trapped in relating dualistically to God only as an other. The prayer that is perfect, in which there is no realization of self or self-reflection about anything, even that you are praying, begins when there is nothing—no word, thought, or symbol—in your prayer. When you no longer realize yourself or the fact that you are praying, you open to God's Trinitarian nature, which is not a thing that can be objectified in consciousness but the reality in which all of life exists. Anthony's perfect prayer is pure contemplation, accessed in centering prayer when you practice with the sacred nothingness.

You orient yourself to Anthony's perfect, or pure, prayer every time you let go of the interior storyline in centering prayer, every time you sit through a period bombarded by thoughts yet remain patiently waiting upon God, trusting in God, trusting that you are already *in God* without relying on tangible experiences *of God*. Not realizing that *you* are praying means that *God* is praying, awakening, in you. Not realizing that you are praying means that the workings of your intellectual mind are unknown or secret from your awareness and from the self who lives behind reflective thinking. Anthony's perfect form of prayer—pure contemplation—shifts you away from having your identity defined by your thoughts and thinking. With pure contemplation, Descartes's famous statement about how intellectual ability defines humankind's sense of self and existence, "I think, therefore I am," is enfolded by a greater truth, a greater realization wherein your sense of who you are is found, lost, and rediscovered in the living mystery of God. Perfect prayer is not about realizing yourself; perfect prayer is about God realizing Godself—the Trinity—in you.[2]

John of the Cross says that the path of contemplation is characterized by *nada,* a Spanish word that, in English, means "nothing." John stresses that on the journey to union with Christ you hang onto nada, nothing—no spiritual experience, no gift, no consolation, no thought, no symbol, no form. After long practice of nada, of letting go of everything, you reach the summit of union with God, in which he says there is—guess what?—nada! Even union with Christ is colored by nothing.

What does John of the Cross mean? He means that in union, God is no thing—not an object of the mind, a thought, or a dualistic experience. In union you realize how God abides in you as the ground from which all things, all objects, all thoughts, and all experiences come. In union there is nothing to hold onto, nothing to claim as your own, nothing that the intellect, memory, or will can affix to, even and especially the dualistic experience of God as something outside you.

But John writes that union with Christ is also characterized by *toda de nada*—"*all* in the *nothing.*" This *toda*, this *all,* this everything that is in the nothing, doesn't take away the nothingness. Rather, the all is a radiant mystery shining within the terms of the nothingness, everywhere and all the time. The *all* that is *nothing* is the effulgent ground of being from which all things are birthed. Union with Christ means oneness with the unseen and hidden ground of everything, a union that unites every separate thing. But because humans are so focused on single, visible separate things we tend to miss out on the unseen and secret source of everything. Jesus invites us to remember the source of everything when he says, "I am the vine, you are the branches. Those who abide in me and I in them bear much fruit, because apart from me you can do nothing" (John 15:5). The all of God is nothing because it is no one thing. The all of God is everything, or, better said, every separate thing comes from God.

How do you open yourself to this kind of union? By praying on God's terms, not your own. Pray with nothing—no thought, no symbol, no effort, no image. Pray only with God. Pray in God, for the Trinity is the all from which everything arises and who is also no thing.

In practicing centering prayer, you normally return, by a symbol of consent, to the presence and action of God. Your word, your breath, or your glance is the direct and definite thing, the symbol in your mind that represents your consent to God's mystery. But as you really begin to understand centering prayer and attune your practice to pure contemplation, you learn how to let go of all symbols, recognize God's presence and action more directly, and consent to that presence. The symbol gets in the way of God when it is just another thing. In the pure contemplation toward which centering prayer orients you, there is nothing between you and God, not even your experience of God. Union is with the Creator, rather than with created things cut off from their source. In the full union into which you are invited by pure contemplation, you relate more freely with everything that springs forth rather than with any single thing. All of human life, every person with whom you are in relationship, every joy, every sorrow, all of your memories and desires, all of your abilities and your failures arise from the all of God, the Creator and source of life. Yet all these things are nothing on their own. Pray with nothing, *nada*, so that you find all, everything—*toda*—in God.

By practicing centering prayer with the sacred nothingness, instead of with a sacred symbol as the object of your prayer, you consent directly to God. In a way, God is the object of your consent; however, this is only an analogy, for objectifying God, turning God into a thing, is exactly what pure contemplation doesn't do. As you move deeper in contemplation and symbols drop away, so too does the subject–object way of relating, knowing, and being. As we shall see, the self-subject and thought-object dualistic ways of relating are replaced in your conscious experience by the Trinitarian life of God, which is not a dualistic experience and does not even manifest interiorly as a dualistic structure of consciousness.

Consider your own experience as a practitioner of centering prayer, as a meditator in any tradition, or just as a human being. Consider those times when, as a fruit of your consent to the mystery of God, you are awake, alive, and fully present to the moment without thinking about being awake, alive, or present. There is no self injecting itself into the experience, no thought interfering with your intuitive experience of the moment. What is there when there is no thought, no thing? There is just an open, loving presence in you, ready to respond compassionately to life, spontaneously, in wonder and in joy. This is a hint of what God's presence is like when it is the subject of your being rather than the object of your thought or experience. Consider what it would be like to return, ever so gently, to that presence, that open awareness, that awakeness, and to have that life live itself in you, more and more, in selfless freedom. Such is the flavor of practicing centering prayer with the sacred nothingness. This way of prayer is difficult to describe, for it doesn't feel like prayer. However, because God is so close, the source of life itself rather than an object outside of you, pure contemplation is actually natural to your experience.

Relating with God directly, without the mediation of a symbol, is pure contemplation. But your time spent consenting to God, indirectly through the mediation of a sacred symbol, helps you learn how to relate directly to God. A swimmer who rests on a life preserver while moving out into the deep end of the pool learns what it is like to rest in the buoyancy of the water. At some point, the swimmer lets go of the life preserver and rests directly, floating, in the water. In the same way, in practicing centering prayer with the sacred nothingness, you learn to practice with a symbol in a receptive way, so that you can practice even more receptively without it and relate directly to the life of God itself. Pray with no thing.

As another great desert father, Evagrius Ponticus, said, "Let me repeat this saying of mine . . . happy is the spirit that has attained to perfect formlessness at the time of prayer."[3] Perfect formlessness is the purest form of prayer—prayer without forms, words, images, or the self as the subject of the prayer. There is just God, who is Trinitarian rather than a thing. God is a mystery that cannot be contained in dualistic experience or thought. God is sacred nothingness to the dualistic mind. Why not align your practice of centering prayer with God?

Centering Prayer with the Sacred Nothingness

I want to pause here and emphasize that this explanation about centering prayer with the sacred nothingness is meant to sow seeds of recognition in you rather than plans or strategies. "Doing" this way of deepening centering prayer is simply a matter of *recognizing what is happening in you during pure contemplation.* As you more consciously recognize what is happening in you, what is happening in you happens more easily! And even if your prayer is not yet stable in pure contemplation, the essential point to remember is that the sacred symbol is just a starting point, a way of consenting to God that opens you to God consenting in you.

With those caveats in mind, let's explore the "practiceless practice" of centering prayer with the sacred nothingness, so that pure contemplation can arise into your consciousness more easily.

To practice centering prayer with the sacred nothingness, you begin by learning how to return ever so gently to God's formless presence. What is God's formless presence? You cannot experience God directly, but the radiance of God's formless presence is sometimes experienced as interior silence, interior stillness, or interior spaciousness. In the absence of attachment to thoughts, the inner faculties are deeply quiet, unmoving, and vast. You are awake to an aspect of the indwelling divine life—the Mind of Christ, God's presence in pure awareness or the Heart of God—and are aware of it as interior silence, stillness, or spaciousness. The practice is to learn to let go of your word, breath, or glance; recognize silence, stillness, or spaciousness; and return to it as you let it return to you. You learn to let a radiance of God's formless presence, experienced through silence, stillness, and spaciousness, live in you as your prayer.

The same contemplative attitudes that you practiced earlier in relationship with the sacred symbol—such as gentleness, effortlessness, letting go, letting be—are still with you as you relate to God more directly, unmediated by any symbol. It is as if your practice of consenting to God with the sacred symbol through, with, and in these contemplative attitudes created grooves in your inner life. These channels of gentleness and receptivity still exist when you allow the Spirit to pray in you without any symbol. All your training with centering prayer ripens into pure contemplation as you let go of your sacred symbol, consent more directly to God's presence, and allow the Spirit to pray in you through the contemplative attitudes that are now worn into your soul. Then, as we shall see, you go deeper into pure contemplation as the Trinitarian life of God awakens into your consciousness and you lose the awareness of God as a thing, an object of your mind. The experience of silence, stillness, and spaciousness disappears and God just is. As the Trinity becomes the true source of your prayer, you also lose the sense of God even as a subject of your mind and life.

There is nothing that you do at this point—no effort, no awareness of acting in any way. As pure contemplation defines more of your prayer, the Christ life in you, the sense of a subtle, true self within falls away. There is only God, who is sacred nothingness to the dualistic mind. Out of this revelation of God comes everything. As we shall see, interior silence, stillness, and spaciousness, beyond the "thingness" of the sacred symbols, are entries into God's sacred nothingness. But they are only doorways; they are not God, and they do not even express the deepest form of contemplative prayer.

Practicing centering prayer with the sacred nothingness takes all the training you have done to much deeper levels. Pure contemplation is a very subtle orientation into which you can awaken at any time. Yet realistically, until you are established in the stable spiritual stage of the transforming union, you will need some support to remain receptive to the state of pure contemplation. That's what centering prayer is all about: it is a simple way of disposing yourself to the grace of contemplation and a simple way of uniting your own actions in prayer with God's presence acting in you. You prepare yourself for the sacred nothingness by practicing with a sacred symbol.

Let's take a moment to look more specifically at how practicing centering prayer with a symbol and how practicing centering prayer with the sacred nothingness interact. If at the beginning of a prayer period you are able to move or awaken into contemplation directly, you don't even need to introduce the sacred symbol. Often, however, even if you have been on the contemplative path for many years, you benefit by temporarily introducing the sacred symbol in order to stabilize your consent to God when you are thinking about thoughts and feelings, just as when you are swimming in heavy waters you may need to hold onto a life preserver to help you find your sense of buoyancy. When practicing centering prayer with the sacred nothingness, you have the sacred symbol available to you as a temporary way of establishing your consent, a consent that you may no longer need as you move into pure contemplation.

So you begin your actual centering prayer period by introducing your sacred symbol. Then continue with the basic instruction for centering prayer: when engaged with your thoughts, return ever so gently to your sacred symbol. Receptivity arises. As you become less engaged with your thoughts and God's indwelling presence begins to enfold your conscious experience, you let the sacred symbol go and continue practicing centering prayer with the sacred nothingness, without any symbol, without returning to the symbol. You let go of the life preserver and just float.

A subtle shift happens. Now, when you are engaged with your thoughts, return ever so gently to God's silence, stillness, and spaciousness. You return effortlessly to God, not to the thingness of your symbol. The "groove" of effortlessness is no longer worn in relation to your symbol, but in relation to God's silence, stillness, and spaciousness. Once you have discovered, or been discovered by, the buoyancy of the Spirit, you float in God and learn to return to the sense of floating, even in heavy waters.

Theologically, centering prayer with the sacred nothingness is a practice of pure hope. John of the Cross says, "that which a person must do in order to live in perfect and pure hope in God is this: As often as distinct ideas, forms and images occur to him, he should immediately, without resting in them, turn to God with loving affection, in emptiness of everything remember-able."[4] According to John's teaching, in contemplation the memory, intellect, and will are purified through the infused gifts of hope, faith, and love. Through this purification, you realize how your identity, your being, and your life itself are created in the image of God. Letting go, forgetting every thought, every thing, even every symbol in centering prayer, in order to turn to God alone, is the way of pure hope. Forgetting past and future opens you to eternity breaking into linear time. The tradition of mystical theology that undergirds centering prayer encourages you to let go of every thing and move into the "cloud of forgetting." *Pray with no thing.* Let your centering prayer move into practicing with the sacred nothingness of God. Let your prayer be of pure hope—pure because it doesn't rely on specific memories, concepts of the future, or thoughts of the past, only on God's formless mystery. Pure hope is right now, right here, like God.

Let Christ Pray in You

Pure contemplation is much more than just letting go of all things, much more than letting go of thinking about thoughts. With contemplation, you participate in the life of God. As we saw in the last chapter, this includes participating in kenosis—Christ's self-emptying. The discipline of centering prayer is self-emptying, self-sacrificing, letting go of the limited sense of self that is separate from God, from others, and from all life. You do this by letting go of engaging with every thought, with your sacred symbol, and with spiritual experiences.

At some point, you reach the limit of your own ability to let go, and Christ lets go within you. To reach true transformation in Christ, you surrender into his sacrificial life within. The mystery of sacrificial love, Christ's kenosis, is inscribed in time through his passion, death, and resurrection, when Jesus gave his life in self-emptying love to the Father for all humankind. As a Christian practitioner, your own letting go, your kenosis, is mirrored in Christ's letting go, his kenosis in you. Pray in God; actively practice kenosis while also receiving Christ's kenosis within.

Through your own and Christ's deep self-emptying, God gradually comes to live in you as the subject of your prayer and, gradually, your life. As we have seen, you begin to understand Paul's statement "I live, not now I, but Christ lives in me" (Galatians 2:20) not as a description of an experience, but as a description of the way inner experiencing and consciousness are being restructured in you. When Jesus is not constrained as only an object of devotion, Christ is able to become the subject of your prayer and your life, in pure contemplation.

Mother Teresa of Calcutta, in her direct and simple way, spoke of the inner dynamics of pure contemplation. She acknowledged that it doesn't feel like prayer, because it is really Christ's prayer in you. She wrote, "And when times come when we can't pray, it is very simple: if Jesus is in my heart let Him pray, let me allow Him to pray in me, to talk to His Father in the silence of my heart."[5] At times when you can't pray, let Jesus pray in you to the Father. Let your heart be silent. This is pure contemplation. There are no words or images or efforts in pure contemplation, for it is Christ's prayer to his Father coming to life in you on a very subtle level. This most profound kind of prayer, which may not feel like prayer, is the source of transformation in Christ. In order to allow Christ to pray in you to the Father, pray with nothing. Pray in God.

How do you *do* this? Trust in your deepening experience of God. Self-empty in love. Let your prayer be found in God. Centering prayer sets you on the path toward this realization when, in its basic guidelines, it says, *Consent to the presence and action of God within.* Practicing centering prayer with the sacred nothingness lets God's presence and action find you. Be found, more and more, in God.

Perichoresis: Dancing in God

This greater mystery of how your prayer and your life are imaged in God is described by another Greek word: *perichoresis. Perichoresis* is the Greek theological term that describes the eternal, infinite, loving flow between the persons of the Trinity: Father, Son, and Holy Spirit. In more colloquial theology, *perichoresis* is sometimes translated into English as "dancing," referring to the interconnected, self-gifting dance of the Divine Persons.[6] Within the inner life of the Trinity, each person fully receives and is given to the other. Through this movement, the inner life of God is revealed as unitive. The Son is given fully to the Father. The Father is given fully to the Son. The Spirit is the gift of love between the Father and the Son and the eternal gift arising out of the Trinity as the animating force of the world. The inner self-gifting of the Trinity is an unseen mystery, yet the Word made flesh in Christ makes perichoresis visible.

This eternal self-gifting is made manifest with the Father's gift of the Son into the world in the Incarnation, with the Son's sacrifice of himself into the Father's embrace in the Crucifixion, and with the gift of the Spirit out of the Trinity to the world at Pentecost. The contemplative teacher Cynthia Bourgeault uses the metaphor of a waterwheel to hint at what the perichoresis of the Trinity is. As the buckets of the waterwheel are drawn upward and over its top, they self-empty into the next bucket, providing energy for the wheel so that the next bucket reaches the top and self-empties into the next.[7] The bucket has no function on the waterwheel but to give its water away. If it retains its water, the wheel stagnates. Within the Trinity, each person—Father, Son, and Spirit—remains distinct. Yet because the love inherent in the nature of God is so vast, there is no fixed point of reference for the divine self-identities. The persons of the Trinity live in each other, three and one, while still remaining distinct persons.

In pure contemplation, you realize your own human participation in the divine perichoresis, in God's inner life, in Christ's self-gifting to his Father, in the Spirit. As you deepen in contemplation, the image and likeness of God in which you are created (Genesis 1:27) suffuses your conscious life. The self that defines your superficial identity, separate from God, is discovered in union with Christ's gift of his self to the Father. The Divine Persons live their dancing, their perichoresis in you, and your own sense of who you are is brought from the manifest to the subtle. Who are you? Created in the image of God, you are a self-gifting. As you give yourself away, there exists no fixed point of reference for your self. Christ's love arises spontaneously from within you as part of the self-gifting. You discover your true personhood in union with God, other people, and all of creation, not in the contracted illusion of the separate-self sense. In order to find your life, you must lose it—you must give it away, in God.

What do you do in this way of prayer? In your surrender, you consent to God's presence and action. In your self-emptying, you let Christ pray to the Father. Jesus's request of his disciples in the garden of Gethsemane, "Sit here while I pray . . . wait here and keep awake with me" (Matthew 26:37–38), takes on new meaning in the light of pure contemplation. You sit in centering prayer, waiting, awake, so Christ can pray in you and in all things. As Anthony of the Desert said, "The prayer of the monk is not perfect until he no longer realizes himself or the fact that he is praying."

Earlier in this chapter, we explored how centering prayer with the sacred nothingness is a way of pure hope, in which we let go of forms and images in order to pray to God alone. Pure contemplation, in which we realize our prayer in God's Trinitarian life, is also a way of *pure faith*. Thomas Keating says, "The way of pure faith is a giant leap of spiritual development beyond the level of those who seek enlightenment or spiritual consolation . . . pure faith is a movement beyond the limitations of our attachments."[8] Pure faith doesn't rely on experiences of God. John of the Cross says over and over again that attachment to spiritual experiences is what keeps us from full union with God. By attaching to consoling experiences of God, or by resisting difficult experiences, we remain focused on things, stuck on the surface of contemplative practice, the surface of relationship with God, the surface of life.

When you pray with no thing, in pure faith, you let God come alive in your prayer so that Christ is no longer the object of your prayer, but the subject praying. When you let go of every spiritual experience, even your relationship with Christ, you enter into the deepest movement of faith. What does pure faith mean, practically? It means to continue in the ordinariness, the dryness, the emptiness of your daily contemplative practice. Realize ordinariness, dryness, and emptiness as just things, arising from their secret source. Let *nada,* nothing, become *toda,* the source of everything. Just sit and wait with Christ praying secretly in you. Trust that you are in God and that God is in you.

Committed to letting go of forms and listening in absence, you will hear the music of God's silence. Waiting, without moving from your prayer spot, during times of dryness, you will perceive the divine stillness. Just being in God amidst contracted self-isolation, you will be seen in the vast spaciousness of God.

CHAPTER SEVEN

The Sacred Nothingness and the Trinity

On that day you will know that I am in my Father
and you in me and I in you.
—John 14:20

Once you awaken to pure contemplation through the prayer of sacred nothingness, the question arises: what happens next? Is there a next? Paradoxically, everything is complete in the present moment in God, and there is also always more on the spiritual journey. As Gregory the Great says, the contemplative path is a journey "from glory to glory." In pure contemplation, pure hope and pure faith are brought to completion by something greater.[1] In order to explore what comes next, let's turn from theology to story—the brief story of a question, really. This question and its answer shed light on the ongoing journey of pure contemplation and the paradox of contemplative practice.

Moving beyond Self-Awareness

I was rather quiet during the centering prayer intensive retreat I was on with Father Thomas Keating (which I describe more fully in Chapter 10). His teachings on centering prayer affirmed the path I had been following, and I was content to receive them silently. However, as the two-week retreat unfolded, a new question formed in my mind. In the time leading up to the retreat, my centering prayer began to include more and more interior silence. I was experiencing a kind of encompassing inner stillness filled with God's empty spacious presence, without any thoughts or movement toward thinking or reflecting. But I also recognized that there was something behind these experiences, a subtle, hidden veil of self, that I thought was a barrier to my abandonment to God.

I wasn't sure if I could accurately speak of it. I remember vividly the scene on that retreat. Our small group of retreatants, twelve of us, were sitting with Father Thomas in a circle around a low table in an adobe room in the retreat center, reclining somewhat on cushions. The scene was rather biblical! Father Thomas had given his prepared teaching and now opened the circle to questions. A few of the other retreatants, the extroverts, made comments first. Then I spoke. The question-and-answer sessions of that retreat were tape-recorded, and our exchange was later incorporated in his book *Open Mind, Open Heart*.

> *David:* Sometimes I have no thoughts. There is only my self-awareness. I don't know whether to let go of it or to be aware of it.

> *Father Thomas:* That is a crucial question. If you are aware of no thoughts, you are aware of something and that is a thought. If at that point you can lose the awareness that you are aware of no thoughts, you will move into pure consciousness. In that state there is no consciousness of self.[2]

Father Thomas saw through my inarticulateness and offered me words of wisdom. His few words clarified how something in me, the subtle self-awareness that witnesses the deepest states of prayer and meditation, could be an obstacle to full union with God. He helped me recognize how a much more subtle aspect of God was coming to life in my centering prayer. My meditation periods during the rest of the retreat were blessed by something new, as difficult to speak about as my question. I had a new sense that for the fuller development of pure contemplation, it is critical to move from the awareness of deep interior silence into *pure consciousness,* in which there is not even an indirect sense of self that is conscious of being aware. Interior silence, stillness, spaciousness, and the absence of thoughts, valuable that they are, are experiences in consciousness, not pure consciousness itself.

The experience I asked about is the same as the prayer of union referred to at the end of Chapter 5 on deepening the sacred glance. Recall that in the prayer of union your thoughts, thinking, and all your faculties are united with God, while you remain *fully aware of this union.*[3] Remember, this type of prayer is not union with an object of thought or perception, or even with a spiritual experience of God. This prayer involves uniting with the ground of experience, in which awareness is freed from all thoughts. In the prayer of union, there is a subject who is aware—not the separate-self sense conditioned by thoughts and emotions, but the Christ life who is aware, through you, of his uncreated, unobjectifiable source, the Father. There may be great stillness within, with no thoughts, no things as objects to the mind. But there is a hidden subject who is aware in you, and the separate-self sense subtly identifies with it. You identify with awareness itself and silently witness the contents of awareness, or its lack of contents in a still, silent interior spaciousness.

As discussed in the previous chapter, when you pray *in God,* surrendering all symbols and spiritual experiences in pure hope and pure faith, even to the point where you lose the experience of God as an object of your mind, you realize Christ as the subject, the true self within you, praying in perichoretic love to the Father. In the fullness of pure contemplation, this hidden subject, this spiritual witness, is invited to lose any kind of awareness, any point of subjectivity, as it is fully known in even greater sacred nothingness. Remember Anthony of the Desert's wisdom saying: "The prayer of the monk is not perfect until he no longer realizes himself or the fact that he is praying." The next step in pure contemplation involves a deeper experience of the divine life, a greater oneness, a fuller union.

The Father Knowing the Son in the Ground of Your Being

Teresa of Avila distinguishes a deeper state of contemplative prayer, the prayer of full union. In full union you lose the awareness of union itself. In that state, there is no consciousness of self, no inferred subject who is aware, not even the true self of Christ in relationship with the Father. In the prayer of full union, you awaken to a different side of the divine self-gifting dance. Now you realize a different aspect of the Trinitarian life, in which the Father becomes the subject self-gifting to Christ *beyond any subjectivity or selfhood in you.* In full union, the true self of Christ is lost in the loving gaze of the Father. The silent witness falls away. There may be silence, stillness, and spaciousness, but no longer as objects, as things of the mind. Interior silence becomes silent, not a thing to be experienced. Interior stillness becomes unmoving, not a thing to be experienced. Interior spaciousness becomes infinitely vast, not a thing to be experienced. There is just God.

As Thomas Keating says, in pure consciousness, you lose the awareness that you are aware of no thoughts. The Trinity prays, awakening within you into its fullness, first in the prayer of union, the Spirit moving from Son to Father, and then in the prayer of full union, the Spirit moving from Father to Son. The prayer of full union, manifesting interiorly as pure consciousness, is a state lacking any fixed point of self-reference. There is no subject to this state, for the Father is uncreated, hidden, secret. It is the Son who makes God manifest and who can be united with your own deepest sense of self in the prayer of union. The mystery of the Incarnation, in which the Word was made flesh, reveals God breaking into this human life of joy and sorrow, of linear time and created forms.

After coming into the world, and to us, the Son then leads us into relationship with the Father. Jesus as the Son of God went through death, physical and spiritual. The spiritual death that Jesus went through at his crucifixion involved losing the intimate union that was always his as the Son, his own subjective sense of knowing, of being in relationship with his Father. When Jesus was on the cross, he cried out, "My God, my God, why have you forsaken me?" (Matthew 27:46). These words express the sacrifice of everything in his life and the death of his divine self. It was only after his self-gift to the Father was complete that he was resurrected. Through his physical and spiritual death, Christ opens a path to full union with God for his followers. The spiritual meaning of Jesus's crucifixion and death is about transformation: Christ's sacrifice opens a doorway to our salvation from the pain of the human condition, the separate-self sense. But to realize the fullness of Christ's self-gift, we must be transformed on the spiritual journey ourselves, from union to full union. As the early Christian contemplatives were fond of saying, God became human so that humans can become divine.[4]

In full union, the Son is now resurrected within you, returned to the eternal gaze of the Father, his source, beyond any form or experience that you can perceive through dualistic thought, beyond anything you can recognize through any subject–object way of experiencing with any sense of self. The indirect subject of awareness of God as the ground of your being is what needs to fall away. Because pure consciousness is selfless and subjectless, greater divine compassion is unleashed within, quietly, unobtrusively. As the prayer of full union moves from being a state in centering prayer to a more stable condition in activity, you become more transparent to the Trinity in more and more of life, empty to God's presence acting through your ordinary activities, more compassionate in your presence to others, more accepting of your own humanity.

Of this full union, this deep oneness in the Trinity, Jesus said, "On that day you will know that I am in my Father and you in me and I in you" (John 14:20). That day is now, always, in the eternity of the present moment. Awaken to the eternal mystery of God beyond God, of God in God, right here and now, in your unknowing and forgetting and in the unknowing and forgetting of Christ in you.

Let Everything Be, Just As It Is

But the question remains, how do you do this in prayer? *How do you lose the awareness that you are aware of no thoughts?* How does the prayer of union deepen into the prayer of full union?

The greatest hindrance to realizing your union with God is the thought that you are separate from God. Saying this is important, for speaking about the sacred nothingness of pure contemplation may engender an attitude in which you try to get rid of thoughts or go beyond some state of mind. Actually, nothing is an obstacle to God's love in pure contemplation. At this level of prayer, concern about things and thoughts and what to do merely restimulates the dualistic structures of consciousness. So the best disposition for pure contemplation is to *let everything be*—all thoughts, all reflections, all effort, all lack of effort, all suffering, all bliss, everything. *Let everything be, just as it is, in God.*

When I told Father Thomas on that retreat that I don't know whether to let go of my self-awareness when there are no thoughts or to be aware of it, I was trying to solve the question of self-awareness in meditation by subtle strategy. My two strategies were letting go or just being aware. Although these strategies, letting go and just being aware, are very important contemplative attitudes at more manifest levels of practice, they are not as valuable in pure contemplation as *letting everything be*. In both these subtle strategies, there is still an indirect subject who is letting go, a silent witness who is aware of the awareness. It is you experiencing God's interior silence, stillness, and spaciousness. When Father Thomas said, "If you are aware of something that is a thought . . . lose the awareness that you are aware of no thoughts," he redirected me. His reply went beyond either of my strategies into greater receptivity. His suggestion was that I lose the awareness of any *thing*. In losing this awareness, you lose the whole dualistic way of thinking and move into Trinitarian consciousness, freed from self in the self-gifting love of God, manifesting interiorly as pure consciousness.

How do you lose the awareness that you are aware of no thing? There is no way to *do* it through deliberate effort. You cannot try to lose awareness in contemplation any more than you can successfully try to get to sleep at night. Whatever state of prayer you are in, or not in, the greatest obstacle to pure contemplation is the effort to get there. Just be, in the essence, the spirit of Christian contemplation: "amen." The most basic disposition of Christian prayer, the word that ends all prayers, is the simplest "instruction" for pure contemplation. Amen, so be it, let it be.

Pure Love

Pure contemplation first opens you to deep spiritual awareness and eventually and naturally leads into a more profound union. At first, full union may be experienced as a form of nonconsciousness. Thomas Keating says:

This grace takes away all self-reflection. One is not even aware that one is in this state until it is over. Afterwards, one knows that one has been in a spiritual place that was marvelous. Not only does the Spirit suspend the ordinary reflective faculties, but even suspends the sense of an individual self . . . According to St. Teresa, the Prayer of Full Union does not last long.[5]

With time, this complete non-self-awareness becomes integrated into the fully alert, waking state. Consciousness and non-self-awareness are at one in God at the same time. In both instances, there is no self being conscious, no duality of a self being aware of no thoughts, no things, nada. In the path of centering prayer, the way to *toda de nada* is, in a sense, greater nada. Praying with no thing, letting everything be, in God, reaches a fullness that is ever-present. The kingdom of heaven is here, now.

When you pray with no thing, everything finds its own natural place, in God. When you let the Creator of life be the complete source of your existence, all creation is restored to its original balance in you. When you practice centering prayer with the sacred nothingness, all thoughts find their natural release in God. "Perfect formlessness at the time of prayer" not only means that you don't need any dualistic method, form, or symbol to get to God; pure contemplation also means that there is ultimately no obstacle to being in God. When you just are in the sacred nothingness, without any symbol or form as a dualistic object to stimulate your effort and your identity as a separate-self subject, the Trinity enfolds everything. With greater nothingness, the simple presence and spontaneous action of love remains.

In pure contemplation, pure hope and pure faith deepen into pure love. John of the Cross says that selfless love or charity "too causes a void in the will regarding all things . . . A man has to withdraw his affection from all in order to center it wholly upon God."[6] In pure love, receptivity reigns. Let your will go and just be with all things. Rather than making an effort to lose awareness, the self behind self-reflection, just be. John's advice is to practice pure love by voiding the will regarding all things, even the awareness of nada, nothingness. A positive way of saying this is, simply, *let everything be, in God.* In pure contemplation, the Trinitarian perichoretic dance of self-gifting awakens in you as pure love.

The question I introduced at the beginning of this chapter—is there more to the practice of contemplation?—has to be answered in paradox and mystery and experience. Trying to express the paradox of what *practicing* pure contemplation is, Thomas Merton writes:

> When the next step comes you do not take the step . . . what happens is that the separate entity that is *you* apparently disappears and nothing seems to be left but a pure freedom indistinguishable from infinite Freedom, love identified with Love. Not two loves, one waiting for the other . . . And here, where contemplation becomes what it is truly meant to be, it is no longer something infused by God into a created subject, so much as God living in God and identifying a created life with His own Life so there is nothing left of any significance but God living in God.[7]

The paradox of contemplative practice is love, nondual love, pure love. At the edge of pure contemplation, by *letting everything be, just as it is, in God,* you are "practicing" love, pure love. There is a wonderful freedom here, for even if you do not feel like you are at the edge of pure contemplation, your attitude of letting everything be, just as it is, in God, your practice of *amen*, expresses pure love. You are there because God is here, always!

Back to the Basics

Once, as I was teaching a basic introductory class on centering prayer, a young woman was confused about the receptive nature of centering prayer. During the question-and-answer period, she said, "Sometimes I am not distracted by my thoughts. There is only my sacred word. I don't know whether to let go of the sacred word or to keep returning to it."

I responded, "If you are continually returning to the sacred word, you are relating to a symbol, not God. If at that point you can lose the sacred word, you will move into contemplation. In contemplation there are no words or symbols for God."

This answer helped her ease into the paradox of action and receptivity in centering prayer. But what struck me about my reply was how familiar it sounded. I remembered Father Thomas's answer to my own question, years earlier. His guidance had shaped my prayer, and my prayer shaped the way I answered this young woman's question. How might this young woman "lose" the sacred word? By not trying to lose it; by letting the sacred word be, just as it is, in God; by letting the meaning of *amen* infuse her practice of centering prayer.

This young woman's question made me realize two things: first, there is a difference between centering prayer and pure contemplation; second, there is also a striking similarity between them. The difference is that in centering prayer you begin by relating to a symbol through active attitudes, such as gentleness, and in pure contemplation you begin by relating to the awareness of God through much more receptive attitudes, such as effortlessness. The similarity is that in centering prayer, you allow the symbol to fall away, and in pure contemplation, you also allow the awareness of God to fall away.

When I answered her question about the basic practice of centering prayer, I realized how profound this simple practice is.

Learning how to practice centering prayer helps shape us for pure contemplation. Experiencing pure contemplation informs our practice of centering prayer. Centering prayer and pure contemplation are different, but similar, aspects of Christian prayer. Each informs and complements the other. Practicing centering prayer with the sacred nothingness brings us closer to the gift of pure contemplation.

CHAPTER EIGHT

Dancing in the Center of God

When you pray, go to your inner room, close the door,
and pray to your Father in secret. And your Father
who sees in secret will reward you.

—Matthew 6:6

Contemplation is a lot like dancing. A dance has different steps and different movements that bring you into deeper relationship with your partner. In the divine dance that is contemplation, you are drawn into a more subtle relationship with Christ, a relationship of oneness, of union beyond duality. Out of this growing inner union, you learn to move in unity with God's emergence in life. As John of the Cross says, the soul's center is God. Because God is also the center of the universe, union with God in the depths of your being unifies you with everything that exists. Learning to dance with God in prayer reveals the hidden movements, the secret choreography of life itself.

Let's look at seven deepening movements of the dance with God: preparing, orienting toward your partner, relating, yielding to your partner, handling challenges, uniting with your partner, and expressing the dance in life. Each of these movements is related to one aspect of Jesus's wisdom-saying on the prayer in secret (Matthew 6:6), the scriptural basis for all of these teachings on centering prayer and contemplative practice.

101

Movement 1: Preparing

When you pray, go to your inner room, close the door,
and pray to your Father in secret. And your Father
who sees in secret will reward you.

Every dance requires preparation, limbering up, readying body and mind. Before getting out on the floor, you need to put on your dance shoes. Preparation is also required for the divine dance of contemplation. In his teaching on the prayer in secret, Jesus affirms the values of preparation when he says, "When you pray, go to your inner room and close the door." Letting go of externalities helps you prepare for relating with God in the secret, interior relationship of contemplation.

As we have seen, for centering prayer, preparation includes readying your body posture and intention. You assume a body position that is alert, natural, and receptive, with eyes closed. You silently introduce your sacred symbol, which you have chosen as an expression of your intention to consent to God's presence and action within. These are the first basic guidelines of Thomas Keating's teachings on centering prayer.

The practice of the sacred nothingness also includes preparing your body and intention in the same way, though this practice can be done more easily with your eyes open. When your practice is consenting directly to God, without a word, breath, or glance, there is also nothing that interferes with God's presence consenting in you, no thought or perception or image. Keeping your eyes open in the practice of the sacred nothingness helps some people realize God's presence acting as the source of all life. When practicing centering prayer with the sacred nothingness, you can introduce a sacred symbol for a few moments. You can practice with interior silence, stillness, or spaciousness. Briefly preparing with a word, your breath, or a glance renews your intention and stabilizes your consent before you let the symbol go into the sacred nothingness of God.

Your active consent in centering prayer and the receptivity to God's presence consenting in you blend together, enriching your prayer practice. Prayer and practice ripen into a greater whole as your yes is more aligned with God's yes. But there is a real self-emptying involved in this preparatory movement of the divine dance. You need to generate your intention while also opening to the source of contemplation, the Trinity present and acting within you.

Movement 2: Orienting Toward Your Partner

When you pray, go to your inner room, close the door,
and pray to your Father *in secret. And your Father*
who sees in secret will reward you.

Once you have put on your dance shoes and prepared your body and your intention, the next thing to do in beginning a dance involves turning toward your partner. As the dance deepens, it is important that you remain oriented toward your partner. When Jesus says, "and pray to your Father," he invites you to orient yourself inwardly, attuning yourself, disposing yourself in the movements of prayer to his secret source, his Father, who is now available to you as your Father, your secret generative source. Jesus's instruction to "pray to your Father" is the first step in introducing you to the perichoresis, the divine dance, of the indwelling Trinity.

Centering prayer gives you a tangible support for this secret relationship by providing you with a form, a temporary intermediary to which to orient yourself: your sacred symbol. Your symbol orienting you toward "consent" to God can be the sacred word, the sacred breath, or the sacred glance. As we have seen, each has certain possibilities, benefits, and attractions for different people during different seasons of the spiritual journey. Whatever symbol you choose, it helps orient you to God, your partner in the divine dance, until you rest in oneness beyond the symbol. Thinking about other thoughts is like looking at other dancers or thinking about other dance steps. In centering prayer, you practice the active attitude of simplicity and stay with *this* partner, *this* dance, by returning to your sacred symbol rather than engaging with your thoughts.

In the practice of the sacred nothingness, you orient yourself not to a symbol, but to the formless mystery of God. How do you do this? By awakening to the sacred nothingness of God. God exists beyond and beneath and within the tangible *things,* the objects and forms of your thoughts. God's presence is always present within, as the ground of awareness in which the forms of your thoughts come and go. It is not your separate-self sense that orients toward God's sacred nothingness. Rather, God awakens in you. Let God awaken in you in sacred nothingness, the secret life that exists within everything in your mind. If you are practicing contemplation, this is the inner reality to orient toward or, better said, *be oriented in.* It may take some time and some subtlety to recognize God's formless, interior presence. That is why aligning yourself with the grace of Jesus's teaching and having an introductory practice like centering prayer is helpful. But you can be found in the ever-present sacred nothingness of God at any time. Like when you are roused from a dream into the illumination of morning, all that is required is that you awaken to God's clear, radiant light.

As you learn to remain with the simplicity of your practice, without contaminating it with extraneous strategies that come to you in the form of engaging with thoughts, you awaken to God's formless presence. There is a real self-emptying involved in this practice. In contemplation, you begin to participate in the divine life in "pure hope," empty of all created images and forms, open to your Father, a mystery of whom "you have never heard his voice or seen his form" (John 5:37).

Movement 3: Relating

When you pray, go to your inner room, close the door,
*and pray to your Father **in secret**. And your Father*
who sees in secret will reward you.

In a dance, once you are oriented toward your partner, you need to be aware of *how* you hold him or her, *how* you move, *how* you relate as your dance deepens. The way you relate to your partner comes alive when you practice secrecy, effortlessness, and gentleness. Secrecy is at the heart of Jesus's teaching on how to pray, for his brief teaching is concerned with relating to God in hiddenness, deep within your "inner room," inaccessible to thought and the ways you identify with thoughts.

In centering prayer, the sacred symbol provides a tangible support for learning how to let go of other forms and realize God's formless eternal presence. But unless you relate *gently* with this symbol, you will remain at the surface of meditation. The key term for relating to God in contemplation is *effortlessness*. There is no striving, no need to act gently when you are relating to the sacred nothingness of God, when there is nothing but God in your prayer. When you are effortless, you let go of all sense of God as a dualistic experience and open to the first aspect of Trinitarian perichoresis: the Son in you praying, self-gifting, to the Father. The practice of the sacred nothingness is Christ's prayer in you, a prayer that unfolds effortlessly, in secrecy, helped when you learn to practice with gentleness in centering prayer, ever so gently returning to your sacred symbol of consenting to God.

Dancing with God is a sacred encounter realized *through* gentleness, *with* effortlessness, and *in* secrecy. Gentleness and effortlessness intermingle in you; activity and receptivity blend in a dance with God in the secrecy of pure faith, empty of all effort, unattached to any spiritual experience, even and especially the apprehension of Christ as an object of your mind. When you hold objects in mind, effort exists, sometimes very subtly, in the separation between you and the object of your perception. Effort brings you out of gentleness, effortlessness, secrecy, and God.

Movement 4: Yielding to Your Partner

When you pray, go to your inner room, close the door,
*and pray to your Father in secret. **And your Father***
who sees in secret will reward you.

When dancing, there is a point when you lose the awareness of yourself, what you are doing, and you give yourself to your partner. The two of you become one in the dance. You *let go and let be* in oneness with your partner.

When Jesus says, "and your Father," he expresses in a pithy way a profound deepening in his teaching. He shifts his simple instruction about how to pray from what you do—praying to your Father, in secret—to what the Father does. The Father, his unseen source, is the reality Jesus invites you to realize as your own unseen source, your own true partner in the dance of contemplation. This realization is not about knowing the Father, but of being known by him, in his self-gifting, his perichoresis, to the Son, in you. When you yield to being known by your partner in the dance, the Trinitarian life is transmitted to you. What was unconscious in you now becomes conscious. This is the gift of Jesus's teaching on how to pray and the gift of himself as the

Christ, the Word of God, spoken by the Father into this world. The prayer in secret is the template for pure contemplation, for deepening centering prayer with a sacred symbol, and for centering prayer with the sacred nothingness.

How does this deepening happen? In the deepening of centering prayer, you let go of your sacred symbol and rest in that which it symbolizes: the formless presence of God. It is this silent, formless presence that the form of your sacred symbol represents and comes from. Your willingness to realize how the sacred symbol arises from God and your willingness to let go of the sacred symbol and be known by God is the hallmark of centering prayer and a primary reason why this contemplative practice is so attuned with Jesus's teaching.

Similarly, as the practice of the sacred nothingness deepens, you also move into a greater experience of God's revelation. In the practice of the sacred nothingness, when you let everything be, just as it is, in God, especially the subtle awareness of your union, you awaken into pure consciousness, in which there is no hidden subject, no spiritual witness who is aware in you. Even the awareness of interior silence, stillness, and spaciousness is brought to oneness in God. The Father knowing the Son within you is the true subject–object relationship that releases you from the pain of the separate-self sense into true personhood, in which the gift of your humanity, created in the image of God's Trinitarian life, is finally realized in the likeness of God. There is nothing to hold onto, no one to be, when you let the perichoresis of the Father to the Son be, in you.

Yielding to your partner in the divine dance of contemplation is a movement of pure love. There is no effort involved in pure love, no self who needs to achieve anything. Pure love involves receiving a reality that already exists within you, a reality—the Trinity—that is comprised of self-gifting love.

Movement 5: Handling Challenges

*When you pray, go to your inner room, close the door, and
pray to your Father in secret. And **your Father
who sees in secret** will reward you.*

What happens when a dancer stumbles? A great dancer has the
skill to perform flawlessly, but also has dexterity, so that when an
unexpected challenge comes, she recovers and even incorporates
the stumble into the dance, as if the misstep were intentional.

Likewise, in the dance of contemplation, nothing is excluded from
the divine life. All that is needed is that you continue relating with your
partner, finding God within the challenge and the challenge within God.
Every aspect of the human condition can be discovered in God, including
the challenges of suffering, despair, doubt, death, illness, and injustice.

When Jesus uses the phrase "your Father, who sees in secret,"
or in some translations, "who is in secret," he is affirming, once
again, the unseen, nondual, and hidden quality of God. Suffering
is a challenge when God is experienced as absent. But because in
Jesus's teaching, God is, *by definition,* in secret, the way to handle
the challenges of the contemplative path is to actually go deeper
into God, through practice that is *more secret,* until you "see" and
experience prayer and life the way God does. In other words, when
you experience suffering on the spiritual path, trust that God is
present and join with God, hidden in the suffering. Don't look for
a dualistic experience of God or hold onto a dualistic concept of
God. Let your experience of God deepen and transform challenges
and suffering.

In these brief words, Jesus affirms that God is unknowable
except by faith—a faith that is not about dogmatic belief that keeps
you safely distant from suffering, but a faith involving deep practice
that transforms your relationship to suffering. Remembering and

trusting that everything—especially suffering and the dark side of the human condition—*is secretly in God* is the way to handle the challenges that arise in the divine dance of contemplation and in life itself. By practicing with God, who sees and is in secret, suffering becomes part of the dance itself, rather than something that is resisted because it is unexpected or unwanted. Of course, seeing suffering as secretly in God is not so easy. Pain and suffering are a part of life—sometimes big parts. So you need a practice for handling challenges on the spiritual path, a simple and ingrained movement in your consciousness that you can turn to whenever suffering arises.

In centering prayer, you realize God's secret presence in suffering when, in faith, instead of following your thoughts about an event, you actively embrace the Spirit within, in the energy of the strong feeling. In the practice of contemplation, you realize God's secrecy when you are embraced by the Trinitarian life during dread, emptiness, the dark nights and the subtle contraction, the attachment and identification of the self in subject–object consciousness. These are two of the simple responses that begin to transform challenges on the spiritual path, one attuned to the emotional qualities of suffering felt on the surface of consciousness and the other attuned to the more subtle qualities of suffering arising from the structure of the separate-self sense, in consciousness.

Movement 6: Uniting with Your Partner

When you pray, go to your inner room, close the door, and
pray to your Father in secret. And your Father
*who sees in secret **will reward you.***

In a dance, after preparing, orienting, learning how to relate to your partner, yielding to your partner, and handling challenges, something more is possible. After executing all these movements, the possibility of oneness with your partner opens up. In this union, there are no longer two dancers, but one dance. Oneness with your partner can be expressed in stillness or in dynamic, free improvisation. From this kind of oneness, all other movements of the dance, all things, arise in a new way.

Jesus's teaching does not say *what* it is that you will be rewarded with, only *that* it is the Father, who is in secret, who *will reward you*. In this discreet phrase, Jesus again suggests secrecy, oneness, transformation, rather than some superficial reward, some answer to a prayer. For when you orient yourself not to a reward, a specific gift, but to the One who gives, who is behind every gift, you are attuning yourself to hiddenness, to subtlety. The fullness of a relationship, the ripening of perichoresis, is fully receiving the other's self-gifting in a union that transforms who you are. Elsewhere in scripture Jesus says, "On that day you will know that I am in my Father and you in me and I in you" (John 14:20). Full union is *being one with God, in God,* beyond duality. Oneness with God, your true and hidden and nondual partner, is the reward of Jesus's teaching on how to pray. Full union is a greater gift than any answer to a single prayer.

Oneness is a gift opened by practicing and resting and being in God. In the practice of the sacred nothingness, just *being, in God,* expresses your orientation toward the Father's reward. Full union is possible when you are just being, fully, in the present moment, with no indirect subject behind your awareness of being. There is no self-referencing in this kind of being. The practice of contemplation involves being beyond being. As self-reflections, self-reflecting, and the self-reflector drop away, there is just God, awakening in you as the Godhead—God the Father in union with God the Son through God the Spirit. This kind of full union is beyond dualistic experience or perception. The closest way of describing its interior effects is as pure consciousness, radiantly empty of all things, yet containing all things, the ground of being shining through everything in the union of the Godhead. The practice of the sacred nothingness opens the door within to the reward of full union with God, free from the self that is indirectly behind self-reflective thought. Centering prayer, especially as it moves into resting and being in God, orients you toward the Father's reward in the prayer in secret.

Movement 7: Expressing the Dance in Life

Our Father who is in heaven, Hallowed be Your name. Your kingdom come. Your will be done, on earth as it is in heaven. Give us this day our daily bread. And forgive us our debts, as we also have forgiven our debtors. And do not lead us into temptation, but deliver us from evil.

—Matthew 6:9–13[1]

The prescribed steps and movements of a dance change how you move in life. So too does the art of contemplation transform who you are, so that you live life aligned more with God, your secret and true partner, in all things.

The final movement of the divine dance of contemplation is that of living union, oneness, in the ordinary events of human life. The fullness of Jesus's teaching on the prayer in secret and union is about unity. Unity is different, greater than union. Union is oneness. Unity is oneness expressed in diversity. Unity is when the divine and human are not separate.

Consider the sequence of Jesus's teaching on prayer in the sixth chapter of Matthew's gospel. First, in the fifth verse, he instructs you *not* to pray like the hypocrites on the street corners, externally, for others to see. He says, "Do not pray like this." Second, in the sixth verse, he says, if you want to really pray, pray *like* this: *in your inner room, in secret, to your Father.* Jesus invites you to contemplation and thereby initiates you into his own experience of God. Third, in subsequent verses, he gives you a specific set of words, the Our Father or Lord's Prayer, the crowning instruction in his teaching on prayer. After speaking about the process of praying in secret, he instructs you in a *prayer in words* about ordinary life.

The Our Father expresses the secret relationship with God in ordinary life. When Jesus's disciples asked him how to pray, he did not immediately instruct them in the words of the Our Father. Instead, he gave them a threefold wisdom saying to lead them into a living relationship with his own Source. The completion of this wisdom-saying is a prayer in words that expresses this secret union in the forms and details of ordinary life. The order in which Jesus presents these teachings on how to pray suggests that you begin by praying in contemplation and then let words and life emerge from the secrecy of union with God. Jesus completes his teaching on union with unity.

How do you realize unity in ordinary life? To give a hint, unity in ordinary life is just that: very simple, very human, very ordinary. Unity is as everyday and familiar as the words of the Our Father. It is as simple as making a living, as simple as forgiveness in relationships, as simple as asking for freedom from spiritual suffering. Life lived in unity does not look special. Unity is expressed in life in ordinary acts of faith, hope, and love; it is acting with compassion in unseen ways; it is acting to alleviate the suffering and injustice of the world.

How do you put Jesus's teaching on prayer and compassionate action into practice? The final movement of the practice of contemplation is about realizing how all things, all thoughts, all actions are emerging into created life out of the secrecy of God. Unity is stabilized in all of manifest life when everything—every prayer, interior thought, perception, and feeling, and every external event, action, and aspect of life—is experienced as emerging in pure consciousness without attachment, resistance, or contraction into the separate-self sense.

Everything Is a Sacred Symbol of God

The fullness of Jesus's teaching on the prayer in secret is that everything can become a sacred symbol. You can recognize the busiest thoughts in your ordinary mind birthing, abiding, and disappearing in God. Just like the words of the Our Father, thoughts become prayers, sacred symbols emerging in the secret prayer of Christ. In the deepest experience of God, which is really not a dualistic *experience* in consciousness at all, you awaken into Trinitarian consciousness itself. There is ultimately no obstacle in prayer and in life when everything is discovered in God.

Jesus's teaching on how to pray, Thomas Keating's teaching on centering prayer, and the practice of the sacred nothingness all describe the movement from duality to union to full union to unity. Our relationship with God is transformed in this divine dance of contemplation.

Why not join in the dance?

PART II

Contemplative Attitudes

CHAPTER NINE

Consent and Giving God Consent to Act in You

Now that you have four ways of deepening centering prayer, let's look at the simple contemplative attitudes common to every way of Christian contemplation. My hope is that these attitudes, like the instructions of Part I, will provide seeds for your own contemplative practice.

How best to begin talking about something as ineffable as God and something as subtle as contemplative practice? The contemplative experience of God is basically inconceivable. Relating to the living God includes saying yes to God's unimaginable indwelling presence. The radical consent of deepening contemplation means something even greater: saying yes to God's presence *acting* in you. As you continue in contemplation, you learn more about how to let God's presence act in you as the source of your prayer and the source of your life. The best way to talk about that is by way of images and stories that give life to insights. So here are an insight, an image, and a story about God and contemplative practice.

The great Christian monk and writer Thomas Merton wrote, "We become contemplatives when God discovers himself in us."[1] This statement goes to the heart of Christian contemplation. Contemplative practice is not something you do to find God. Contemplation involves being found by God. However, there is an even more profound perspective bound up in Merton's statement. You become a contemplative when you allow another to find themselves in you! This finding, happening within you, allows you to be found. Then you can find God. Merton's insight turns us inside out to the mysterious sense of what contemplative practice really is like.

God's discovery of Godself in you is an action so subtle that normally it is only after years of practice that you truly experience the deep ways of grace, the profound sense that everything is in God, and the mysterious ways God acts in you. Merton's statement also points to the delicacy of what you need to do in practice. In an important way, God's discovery of Godself in you is something that happens beyond your own isolated efforts in prayer. God's discovery of Godself in you is a gift unfolding, like a flower that opens on its own, drawn forth by a light you can do nothing to produce or control.

You do need to do something in centering prayer, but this doing is more like being and allowing than self-accomplished busyness. Your activity in centering prayer is like a rose's petals opening to the sunlight, like surrender unfolding inside you, like self-abandonment awakening within. Your action in contemplation is a radical consent to God's eternal nature more than your own self-initiated effort in one contracted moment of time. In an old story, a Zen master tells a student that he, as a human being, is already enlightened, even before beginning the path of meditation. The student asks the master, "If I am already enlightened, why do I have to sit and meditate so much?" The master replies that the sun rises on its own every morning, but if the student doesn't wake up, he will never see the sunrise. This is a wonderful metaphor for contemplation. By practicing, you do not make the sun rise. But by engaging in centering prayer, you can wake up to see the beauty of the sunrise, which dawns on its own.

In Christian practice, contemplation is a matter of sitting down and consenting to the sun rising in you and in all of life. In Christian contemplation, the nature of God and the nature of all of reality is experienced as Trinitarian. This means that the Son—the Logos, the Christ—is continually giving himself to the Father in the movement, in the energy, in the eternal loving exchange between them, which is the Spirit. There is nothing you can do to make this exchange happen. The presence of the Son acts in the Trinity, self-gifting in love to his unseen source, because that is the nature of God. In contemplation, you awaken to this indwelling reality, this gift of love that is the deepest center of your own being and the very heart of the world. In contemplation, you become conscious of God's Trinitarian discovery of Godself. There is nothing you can do to produce or control this presence acting within. It happens because, although hidden, it is God's nature and all of manifest life is mirrored in this nature. You can, however, consciously practice consent to God and learn how consent deepens as you surrender to God's presence acting in you.

You cannot do anything to produce an experience of God in you, but you can say yes to receiving divine love, to awakening to this sacred gift. You can say yes to letting it come into your consciousness and transform the pain of your own contraction, separation, unconscious resistance, and self-isolating behavior. You can be transformed in God's own image, awakening to the sun rising in you. You can let the Son of God shine the light of his love, let the Spirit move a little more freely through you—both radiant to their own unseen source, the Father.

A Struggle with Death and Life

I learned contemplative consent in a profound way at the beginning of my spiritual journey. I have been relearning it, many times, ever since.

My family was not religious and did not speak of God or pray at meals. I remember going to a church only once as a child. Although I knew that my mother had a sense of relationship with God, she kept her faith private. My father lived according to philosophical ethics, but did not relate much to organized religion.

When I was five years old, my mother fell down the basement stairs, broke her back, and began experiencing the constant pain she would endure for the rest of her life. After that happened, an unexpressed existential container began to color my childhood world. Although my life was materially comfortable, what meaning could there be in it if someone as good as my mother could suffer so much?

In 1969, propelled by money and scientific mastery, men walked on the moon. Eleven years old, I watched them on television. That same year, after years of suffering and undone by despair and pain, my mother asphyxiated herself in our garage. Her illness and suicide so shattered any sense of meaning I had that even asking the question "Does God exist?" was irrelevant and unthinkable to me. My life continued in a container of existential despair; it was a life that held an unspoken no to existence, a life absent of meaning.

As I grew older, the search for truth fueled my life. What was the meaning of existence? What was my purpose in life? As a teenager, I studied philosophy in school and read everything I could about the human condition. Although the hippie generation had passed, I still experimented with the secular sacraments of the time: sex, drugs, and rock and roll. Yet these experiences, shared with others, drove me into solitude and nature, poetry and sacred music, away from induced transcendence. I focused my studies on psychology, particularly the emerging transpersonal school, which included the transcendent aspect of human experience. During the day, I worked in a group home with children with developmental disabilities; at night, I worked on campus in a sleep and dream laboratory. I wondered how I could heal my alienation and suffering, how I could awaken from life's illusion.

I discovered Eastern meditation, which brought my search for meaning from theory into practice. Meditation, I found, is based in experience, yet its regular practice transforms the structures of identity and consciousness, the ground from which all experiences and experiencing arise. I tried both Hindu and Buddhist forms of meditation for a while, then settled on Zen Buddhist practice. Rather than espousing a particular dogma, Zen, as it was taught to me then, dealt with my immediate experience and the alleviation of suffering. Zen was the perfect postmodern spirituality for me—a formless path beyond belief. I became a Buddhist existentialist. Rather than following a rigid religious doctrine, I practiced Zen meditation, for two hours each day.

I finished college and, instead of pursuing my doctorate, moved to California to practice Zen with a community and teacher. Once in a while in my meditation I experienced something I had not heard of in Zen. Out of inner emptiness there arose a presence, breaking into me, over me, through me, drawing me in love into greater freedom and a deeper contact with my humanity. Something caressed me; a nameless, ravishing, invisible touch of love breathed life into my hidden despair, into the secret desire for spiritual annihilation that had colored my meditation and limited my compassion, the very purpose and measuring rod of Buddhist practice. When this presence was present, I did not need to know what to do. It was only afterward that the questions came, for the presence was associated not with Asian symbols and means, but with Christian ones. Since I had not been raised as a Christian, I had many questions, and I asked them with all the urgency of a young person's life-or-death struggle for meaning.

My search turned from East to West. In new reading, I learned that the Christian equivalent of Buddhist meditation was called *contemplation* or *contemplative prayer*. Because I had a very nominal exposure to Christianity, the *prayer* I was reading about in the works of writers such as Thomas Merton was something I had never heard of.

I immediately found Merton helpful. Like me, he had gone through, as a young man, a poignant search for truth and for freedom from the pain of the human condition. His parents died when he was young. He attended boarding school and then went to university, first at Cambridge and then at Columbia. He lived a wild life as a young man in England and New York City. He befriended a traveling Hindu swami, flirted with communism, and got a girl pregnant. She died during World War II, in the bombing of London. Merton then went through a spiritual crisis, and he too was touched by the experience of Christ. He eventually converted to Catholicism and became a Trappist monk. In the monastery, his superiors ordered him to use his gifts as a writer. His autobiography became a bestseller, and many of his books became spiritual classics. His words and his life embodied a very human search for the divine with which I identified.

Merton had an ability to articulate what I was experiencing. When asked to describe his prayer, he once wrote:

> Simply speaking, I have a very simple way of prayer. It is centered entirely on the presence of God . . . if I am still present myself, I recognize this as an obstacle. If He wills, He can make the nothingness a total clarity. If He does not will, then the nothingness actually seems to itself be an object and remains an obstacle. Such is my ordinary way of prayer. It is not thinking about anything but a direct seeing of the face of the invisible which cannot be found unless we become lost in Him who is invisible.[2]

As I broadened my reading, I learned that Merton was not writing about an idiosyncratic experience, but expressing the heart of Christian contemplation. Contemplation as a relationship with the mystery of God beyond words was something I could understand because it was something real to me. The Christian contemplative message began to appeal to my mind as well as my experience. It was this understanding of Christ, this living presence, that had found me. It was this mystery that was finding itself in me. It was this God who had awakened my search, this God that was my searching itself. In my Zen practice, my mind was emptied; into this receptive space came Christ's presence and action, God's love and life.

I struggled for some time, wondering about papal authority and crusades, clericalism and fundamentalism, celibacy and dualism. Yet I learned that faith as a living relationship with God included both inquiry and surrender. One night as I walked by the San Francisco Bay, fraught with inner struggle, torn by questions and confusion, a radical consent to the unknown awakened in me. This mystery had come into my life with love, unbidden and unsought. Because at that time it was the Roman Catholic Church, especially in its monastic life, that had preserved the Christian contemplative experience in the West, at the Easter Vigil, in 1981, I responded to God by becoming a Catholic Christian. Like Merton, I had searched for meaning and was found by a truth that surpassed my understanding. Like Merton, I was a convert to consent. After my conversion to Christianity, my daily practice changed from Zen meditation to centering prayer.

Reconversion: The Ongoing Practice of Consent

The Christian contemplative tradition affirms that God's presence acts in you throughout life to transform you on life's journey. Instead of having a single conversion or born-again experience, you need to continue practicing consent to the mystery of God. Centering prayer provides a way of continuing to practice consent. At the time of my religious conversion, the Christian practice of centering prayer was just beginning to be taught outside Roman Catholic monasteries. Reading those first books on centering prayer, I was grateful to find a tradition in Christianity that stressed the need for an ongoing practice in ordinary life and showed a way to do that practice.

In centering prayer, you consent to God's presence and action; in contemplation, God's presence acts in you. Gradually, your consent in practice is permeated by God's yes. Thomas Keating says:

> The only initiative we take during the period of Centering Prayer is to maintain our intention of consenting to the presence and action of God within. This we do by gently returning to the sacred word when we notice we are engaged with thinking some thought, feeling, or bodily sensation.[3]

This description of centering prayer embodies the active contemplative attitude of consent. Consent is an active attitude because it is something you do, an action you take. Just as being married brings the intention expressed in a wedding ceremony to life as a sacred practice, the active practice of consenting, daily, to the mystery of God brings the intention of loving God to life.

I learned that there is a world of difference between being touched by God in an experience and responding to the touch of God by giving my life to the contemplative path through active practice and discipline. A kiss from a lover is a wonderful romantic experience. But where might the kiss lead? Like a kiss that develops into a committed relationship, the touch of God is an invitation to transformation in God, the beloved who is realized as the source of romantic love. Contemplative practice connects you to the source of all love. The path of contemplative transformation is through consent to the beloved, the source of experiences and the source of experiencing itself.

God's Presence Acting in Contemplation

In the beginning of the contemplative journey, the sense that you are separate from God is reinforced by attachment to the thinking process. So every good introduction to contemplative practice involves consenting to God beyond the workings of the intellectual thinking mind. Yet Christian masters like Thomas Merton are clear that there is much more to contemplation than your own actions, on their own. The passage from Merton that I quoted earlier reads, more fully:

> If you succeed in emptying your mind of every thought and every desire, you may indeed withdraw into the center of yourself and concentrate everything within you upon the imaginary point where your life springs out of God: yet you will not really find God . . . [u]nless He utters himself in you . . . speaks His own name in the center of your soul . . . Our discovery of God is, in a way, God's discovery of us . . . We only know Him in so far as we are known by Him . . . We become contemplatives when God discovers Himself in us.[4]

When I was a young man, my Zen meditation practice helped me let go of thoughts in my mind. From this condition, a Zen practitioner would open to the deeper gifts of Buddhist meditation. But because Christian contemplation was my path, letting go of thoughts in my mind did not let me find God. I was brought to my own spiritual path; I was found by God when God's presence acted in me. Over the years, my ongoing spiritual journey has been a humbling relearning of that truth, which was bound up in my original conversion experience.

In scripture Paul says, much more simply than Merton, "It is the Spirit who prays in us" (Romans 8:26). The indwelling presence of God prays in us, acts in us in our prayer, as our prayer. When you learn that all your efforts to pray, to consent to God, to relate with God, are in some sense mere preparations for waking up to the truth that you are already in God, that the Spirit is moving in you in everything you do in contemplative practice, then you are released into a great freedom. The deepest realization of contemplation is not dualistic: you are not separate from and seeking God. God is present in you and acting in all of your life.

Thus, *receptivity to God's presence acting in your prayer* and in your life is a deeper attitude that accompanies the active contemplative attitude of consent. This more receptive contemplative attitude of consent to God's presence acting in you is very important for maturing contemplative practice. In this receptive attitude, the more active contemplative attitude of consent to God, which you may feel like you *do* in your practice, is aligned with God's indwelling nature.

The theological teaching called Trinitarian Exemplarism affirms that God's Trinitarian nature dwells in us, as the ground of our being. The Abba, the Father, the unseen source of life, gives himself to the Logos, the Son, the manifest word spoken out of eternal silence into life, in the love, light, and life of the Spirit. As the Logos gives himself back to the Abba in the Spirit, an eternal cycle of presences acting in self-gifting love vibrates at the heart of all reality. This same cycle resonates in the depths of your own being. Contemplation brings these secret depths to life in you. As the life of God becomes conscious in you, your own self-contracted behaviors are gradually freed into the self-gifting love of God, in simple and ordinary ways appropriate to your unique talents and circumstances of life.

Consent to the Divine Presence Acting in Life

You can practice the contemplative attitudes of *active consent* and *receptivity to the presence of God acting in you* during prayer. You can also practice them in life. Thomas Merton's life story provides a wonderful example of how these contemplative attitudes arise both in prayer and in life.

As a young man, Merton left human society for the separate world of the monastic cloister. There he felt he could pursue his prayer life with God. He gave up writing when he first entered the monastery. He was afraid of his writer's ego and instead gave himself, in pure consent to the mystery of God, to a life devoted to prayer and a monk's simple, manual work.

Then his abbot told him to use his gifts to write. Merton was aghast. But out of monastic obedience to his abbot and his rule of life, he consented. Writing his first book, an autobiography, stimulated his fear of egotism. Could he tell his story in first-person language and not be trapped by his ego? I believe that he was able to write that first book and the many books that came afterward because of the way he practiced the contemplative attitude of consent. The mystery of God was present to him in his vow of obedience. His inner discipline of consent to God's presence and action in prayer helped create the context for the outer consent to God's presence and action in his life. His writing flourished, and the first book, *The Seven Story Mountain,* was a runaway best-seller. He experienced pride about his writing, but because of his contemplative practice, it didn't interfere with his life with God. His vocation as a writer, made and practiced out of obedience, became an expression of his vocation as a contemplative.

Then, after sixteen years in the monastery and many best-selling books on prayer and monasticism, Merton's inner life of prayer and outer life as a writer were turned upside down. During those years, his contemplative prayer had become more receptive to God's presence. His outer life as a man broke open to God's presence acting in it during a revelation that would radically affect his writings from then on. In 1958, Merton wrote in his journal:

> Yesterday, in Louisville, at the corner of 4th and Walnut, suddenly realized that I loved all the people and that none of them were, or, could be totally alien to me. As if waking from a dream—the dream of separateness . . . Thank God! Thank God! I am only another member of the human race, like all the rest of them. I have the immense joy of being a man! As if the sorrows of our condition could really matter, once we begin to realize who and what we are . . . Dear Proverb . . . I shall never forget our meeting yesterday. The touch of your hand makes me a different person.[5]

It was on a busy street corner, not in the monastic cloister, that Merton experienced a transforming shift in his mature perception of God, a changed appreciation of himself and of life. Having left society, relationships with women, and much of his own humanity, Merton experienced God's presence fully alive and active in all these things. His life was never the same again. It took him some years to assimilate the shift that was opened to him on that busy street corner in 1958. He retold the story of this experience in a book published eight years later. But it is in his journal, written the day after the experience in Louisville and published decades after his death, that he alludes to its full impact, especially the way the divine feminine, in the form of an inner experience he named "Proverb" and in the form of women he saw on the street, affected his reconversion to God.

Until the late 1950s, Merton's books were confined to the rarified spirituality of monasticism and contemplation. After the experience at 4th and Walnut, his writing changed. From the deepening solitude of his hermitage, he became passionately involved with the concerns of the world: racism, the nuclear arms race, poverty, the Vietnam War, interreligious dialogue. His writing expressed these concerns. He could not go back to writing books about the monastic cloister.

I believe his writing changed because his inner experience developed. His experience of God deepened. The epiphany on that street corner began to express itself in his life in the world. Where previously his writing was an expression of the active contemplative attitude of consent to God's presence and action in the mystery of his vow of monastic obedience, now Merton's writing was an expression of God's presence acting in him and in the pressing concerns of the world, which were opened up to him in a radical way on that street corner in Louisville.

Even though some of his readers and superiors wanted him to go back to writing only about the cloister, the same relationship that allowed him to write about monastic life allowed him to write about the facets of human life that break forth from the silent divine ground. His commitment to God and to contemplation remained. These deepened through the active contemplative attitude of consent into a more profound attitude that allowed him to receive God's presence acting in his prayer and in his life.

As you recognize and practice these attitudes of consenting and allowing consent to take place in your own contemplative prayer, they express themselves more easily in life outside prayer. Then you become a more open vehicle for the ordinary, unique, surprising, and hidden ways that compassion and love come through you, as an expression of God's presence acting within. The mystery of God leads through solitude into life. Gratefully, I have learned this through my own encounter with the Spirit, animated by the feminine, radiating in the Trinity, inseparable from all manifest life.

It is hard to resist the continual movements of the Spirit of God. When you practice the active contemplative attitude of consent to God's presence and action and the receptive attitude of consent to God's presence acting within and in all life, you are brought into a great freedom. God discovers Godself in you and in all things, and you become a contemplative, both in prayer and in all of life.

Reflective Exercise

Pause for a moment in silence and consider:
- How are you saying or how have you said yes to God?
- When have you found God saying yes in you?

CHAPTER TEN

Opening and Recognizing

How does God help you through your contemplative practice to become more aligned with the divine nature existing within you? How does centering prayer deepen into contemplation? How can you move beyond your own inner obstacles—your sense of effort, struggle, distraction, and emotional turmoil—into the giftedness and gifting of God? The answers to these questions lie not so much in going beyond the obstacles, but in finding God in them and them in God. These obstacles are only a problem when your actions in contemplative practice are separate from God or, better said, when you feel God is separate from your practice and from you. Augustine of Hippo said that God is closer to us than we are to ourselves. Contemplation lets you open to and recognize the closeness of God. God is beyond and between and beneath the inner obstacles that keep you from yourself, from life, and from other people.

Opening is an active contemplative attitude that allows centering prayer to deepen into contemplation. Its counterpart is the contemplative attitude of recognizing. The other, more refined contemplative attitudes described in this book are built upon the foundation of opening and recognizing and will engender even greater receptivity in you.

"To open" means "to untie, unwrap, reveal, or receive." Contemplation is a receiving of the reality of God. "To recognize" means "to be conscious of, admit, or realize." When you *open to* the reality of God, you *recognize* something that was there all the time, something you were not conscious of. Reality breaks through. You see clearly, perhaps for the first time. Contemplation is a gift that you simply open to. God is a continually gifting presence, an ongoing grace that you are invited to recognize in all things, at all times. As your centering prayer practice is infused with the attitudes of opening and recognizing, you see how your actions in the practice of contemplation arise from God and return to God.

You may wonder what these contemplative attitudes look like, more concretely, when they manifest in a person. The Spirit sometimes works through people to reveal something of God's own nature. Often life events, even the most ordinary moments of the day, are what open you to receiving grace. I would like to share a few stories that bring the contemplative attitudes of opening and recognizing to life.

An Icon of Openness

I first spent extended time with Father Thomas Keating during a two-week intensive retreat at the Lama Foundation in northern New Mexico. This retreat center and interreligious community is set on the western slope of the Sangre de Cristo Mountains, overlooking the mesas and gorges of the vast Rio Grande Valley. Twelve people gathered from around the country to listen to Father Thomas teach about the Christian contemplative journey. We also practiced a lot of centering prayer.

When the retreat started, Father Thomas welcomed everyone with his broad smile and genteel hospitality. As the days unfolded, I was struck by a certain patience in him, a generosity of presence. His response to all of us was very accepting. But there was something more in him than just patience. He listened deeply to our experiences and ideas, the ways we connected with his teachings, and the obstacles we encountered. In such deep listening, he heard something of our personhood. From the depths of his very being, he was open to everything. From his centered presence in Christ, he opened to our life stories, our spiritual struggles, our efforts to pray. In doing so, he received us.

As the days went on, I saw how much his mind and spirit were like the sky that encircled us on that mountain. In this expansive sky, clouds appeared and passed. The sun, moon, and stars crossed through it each day. At times, lightning and rain came and went, but the limitless spacious sky remained, opening to everything, receiving all, letting everything go. Father Thomas's spirit was the same. His decades-long commitment to contemplation created the context for me to experience something of God's nature, manifesting through him, through his own gifts, in his own human person. I also found that, in the context of Father Thomas's presence and the New Mexico desert sky, I was better able to deepen my own prayer.

Open Hands

Contemplation awakens you to the resurrected life of Christ, not as an object of thought, but as an ever-present reality within you, beyond you, and enfolding you. This form of prayer is an immersion in the Being of God. Thomas Keating says:

> Saint Thomas Aquinas taught that God is existence and hence is present in everything that exists. If God is present everywhere, it follows that under no circumstances can we ever be separated from him. We may feel that we are; we may think that we are. But in actual fact, there is no way that we can ever be apart from God even if we try![1]

Like the desert sky that holds everything in it, like the mind of a longtime contemplative practitioner, God is the open, receptive ground of everything—all life, all death, all joy, all suffering, all that appears as sacred and divine, all that appears as limited and human.

Opening is a fundamental contemplative attitude for relating to God. You open to the gift of God's indwelling presence and life that is already here, now and always. How you do this depends on the specific contemplative practice to which you are drawn. Every contemplative practice in the Christian tradition creates openness to the ever-present gift of God's life. The basic instructions of centering prayer begin this process of opening to God. The practice of gently returning to your sacred symbol when you are engaged with another thought sets you on the path of openness.

When your hands are open, you can receive a gift someone is offering you. There are many gifts that God gives: faith, love, the ability to serve others, and the ability to pray. Life itself is a gift. Yet the greatest gift of all is God. Contemplative practice cultivates an open-handed disposition toward life and the present moment so you can receive all the great gifts God is showering upon you, including the greatest gift imaginable: God's indwelling presence, the eternal gift toward which you orient and reorient as you progress along the contemplative path.

Particular gifts come and go in life. You are invited to open to difficult things as gifts, too, and you are challenged during times of spiritual darkness not to seek for any particular experiences or tangible gifts other than the subtle presence of God acting within. By orienting yourself toward receiving God as the supreme spiritual gift, you become rooted on the contemplative path and learn to open to everything as a gift. Having open hands is a very apt image for the spiritual journey. With open hands, you are free to receive everything. With open hands, you are also willing to let everything go. In opening to everything and letting everything go, you receive the supreme gift of God, the hidden ground from which all things in life come and to which all things return at death.

Recognizing God in All of Life

My two-week retreat experience with Father Thomas in New Mexico was an exercise in opening. The special conditions of contemplative retreat—silence, intensive periods of contemplative practice, community support, spiritual teachings—were all designed to facilitate receptivity. It worked! On those two weeks in the spaciousness of northern New Mexico, I opened to God in a very deep way. My life was never the same again. The vastness of the desert sky and Father Thomas's presence were great gifts to me.

When I returned to my home in California, I found myself yearning for the special conditions of the retreat. The drabness of my little apartment, the noise, the clutter of the city landscape, and the people I met drained rather than supported me; everything seemed to close my hands and my heart to what I had found and practiced on retreat. When I left my apartment for my first day back at work, I felt closed and contracted. The sky between the concrete buildings was gray and smoggy. Heaviness held my being.

But on my second day home, as I was walking to work, I suddenly noticed a stream of light breaking through the overcast sky. I stood still and just breathed. As I experienced my breath, simply present and breathing in me, the street was illuminated from within with a presence that reflected the light. My heaviness lifted. Freedom came. In that quick moment, something deeper in me, from a place that had been cultivated on the retreat, broke forth in an immediate recognition that everything in my ordinary life—the noise, my feelings of being unsupported, the drabness— was *in God*. As I realized that my breath was always with me, on the retreat and in my city life, my mind and heart opened in a deeper way, a way that included everything. In that instant, I didn't need any special conditions to receive God. Yet at the same time, I also saw how my intensive retreat practice had set something in place in me. I needed the retreat, but the point of the retreat was to help me find God in life. In that flash of recognition, something in me saw that all of life is in God.

I was reminded of the well-known lines from one of T. S. Eliot's more contemplative poems, "Little Gidding":

> We shall not cease from exploration
> And the end of all our exploring
> Will be to arrive where we started
> and know the place for the first time.[2]

There, on the city street that drab, gray morning, as easily as I noticed my breath, I recognized that everything was already in God—both the special conditions that create contemplative openness and everything else that seems so separate from contemplation. There was no separation between grace and ordinary life, nothing special to receive. Everything was all there already, in God.

From the Active Attitude of Opening to the More Receptive Attitude of Recognizing

You can actively practice opening your hands, your mind, and your heart to the gifts God is giving you and to God's presence as the supreme gift. But notice that the action of opening your hands involves moving to create space for something you lack. You *do something* to let go and receive what you don't have. If you have been on the contemplative path for a while, you may find that opening is too active an attitude to describe what is happening in your prayer. The deepest contemplative truth is that grace is already given. God is already here. You just need to recognize that the graced life that has been given you is already here. God's gifting is ongoing, in all things. Recognizing that gifting is like the simple way you recognize your breath in you. Your breath is always here—otherwise you would not be alive. It was given to you at birth; you received it then, and it has sustained your life ever since. But normally you are not aware of breathing. When you simply recognize that you are breathing, then you accept the gift of this moment of life.

Recognizing is the more receptive contemplative attitude, the partner to the active attitude of opening. Normally they go together: practicing opening to God creates space for God to recognize Godself in everything. Sometimes you are opened by life events and simply see the gifting of God that is always here.

Being Still

Christian contemplative practice is a response to God's scriptural invitation to "be still and know that I am God" (Psalm 46:10). You let your mind become still and quiet, intuiting the "peace of God, which surpasses all understanding" (Philippians 4:7). The contemplative knowing of God is an unknowing of any specific concept or thought, because you are the one who is being known. In contemplation, God is less an object of thought than the subject who loves you. This love is not sentimental, not saccharine, but transforming. It is like a purifying flame, burning away all self-sufficient efforts to achieve anything in prayer and, at the deeper contemplative levels, even burning away every effort you make to open. The deepening of contemplation is not doing but simply being, in consent to God's presence and action within.

It is very important to realize that the stillness needed for knowing God is primarily a stilling of your efforts to know God. Too often you create your own obstacles in prayer by thinking that thoughts are a problem, when really it is your unconscious attitude of achievement that is getting in the way. Thinking about thoughts keeps you on the surface of prayer, especially when your thinking is charged with concern and effort. Contemplation is deepening trust and faith that you don't have to go anywhere to find God; you simply recognize the gift of God's love, presence, and Being. The radical nature of opening stills and quiets your efforts to find God in the unmoving, motionless, unknowing faith that you now recognize awakening within.

This is why just sitting still seems to be an essential stance, symbolically and literally, in contemplative practice. Remaining motionless physically and spiritually keeps you receptive to the divine mystery. Consider your own experience: remember a time when you just sat through a difficult period of meditation. The strongest emotions, the emptiest feelings of dryness, the wildest thoughts are enfolded within the commitment to just sit, to be still, to be in naked consent to the unseen mystery of God. The thoughts in your mind do not necessarily go away with this intention to just sit. Wild thoughts may remain. Yet as you just sit still, as you wait in God, a deepening of your consciousness takes place; thoughts are left on the surface of your mind as you disidentify from them. Just being still over time lets the hidden depths of your being—found in relationship with God's eternal Being—come alive to you. Just sitting still lets all your dualistic efforts at achievement, even achieving openness, fall away in the grace of God.

Being Brought to Your Knees

One morning in the middle of Father Thomas's two-week New Mexico retreat, I found I was not feeling well. My stomach was upset and cramped. I looked outside my adobe cell and hailed another retreatant who was passing by. I asked him to tell Father Thomas I was sick and wouldn't be coming to the common events. I settled back in bed under the blankets to rest. After an hour, there was a knock on the door. I opened it to find Father Thomas leaning down from his six-foot-four-inch height to ask through the tiny door how I was. It looked like he was visiting a convalescing hobbit. He offered to get me a homeopathic remedy from his own room. He was so solicitous and kind. When he returned with the medicine, he suggested I pray to God for help and said he would pray for me too. For me, it was as if God had reached through him to me in my illness, touching me in my human need. I took the remedy and went back to bed, where I prayed to God for help. As I surrendered to Christ, my prayer seemed to arise out of the pain itself. Eventually I fell asleep. When I woke, I felt better and rejoined the group for the afternoon period of centering prayer.

The prophet Isaiah says, "The Lord waits to be gracious to you; therefore he will rise up to show mercy to you . . . He will surely be gracious to you at the sound of your cry" (Isaiah 30:18–19). God is not only ever-present ontologically to you, at the ground of your being; God is also present to your human needs, in pain and suffering. Turning toward God is all that is needed for another kind of deepening to unfold in your contemplative practice. The more relational prayer responses of gratitude, petition, and praise—what writer Anne Lamott more simply calls "Thanks," "Help," and "Wow"—build devotion and surrender. Devotion and surrender are indispensable on the spiritual path and greatly augment the radical openness that contemplative practice directly cultivates in you.

The more relational forms of prayer, like gratitude, petition, and praise, are not meant to change or convince God, as if God were indifferent, inattentive, or absentminded. God does not need to hear your cries for assistance to be present to you. These forms of prayer are meant to change you. Gratitude, petition, and praise change you by making you more open to God in your humanity. Just sitting, being still, and knowing that God is God lets you better receive the divine nature already imaged in you. When you become aware of your human nature, in joy, in ordinary life and in suffering, you are invited further into the mystery of God. Relating to God through your human condition is essential. Surrender is needed for the divine life to come into our human life.

In fact, you will never be transformed in God by just sitting still in contemplative openness alone. As Ken Wilber says, the otherness of God, brought forth in surrender, undermines our contracted self-sufficiency like nothing else. Being on your knees is a wonderful symbol of surrender to the Other. The great chant that begins the Trappist contemplative monastic liturgy proclaims surrender to the divine:

> Oh God, come to my assistance,
> Oh Lord, make haste to help me;
> Glory be to the Father and to the Son, and to the Holy Spirit;
> As it was in the beginning, is now, and ever shall be, world
>   without end, amen.

With these words of prayer, the I–Thou relationship is invoked as an entry into the Trinitarian mystery of God that is eternal, beyond linear time. The otherness of God leads into the timeless mystery of God that is too close to you to be other. It just is, here and now.

The two contemplative images of open hands and sitting still are complemented by a third image: being brought to your knees. Have you ever been brought to your knees before God, figuratively or literally? Have you surrendered to God in full acceptance of your human vulnerability and neediness? If so, then your spirituality touches on the incarnational—the divine and the human, present and acting inseparably, in you. The contemplative attitudes open you to the fullness of God, in a very relational way. Learning how to open to this teaching in the experiences of ordinary life, and in the people who come to us as icons—revelations of God's presence—as Father Thomas did to me, is a wonderful gift.

Reflective Exercise

Pause for a moment in silence and consider:

- Which image of opening are you being invited to in your contemplative life: opening your hands, sitting still, or being on your knees?
- How can you better respond to this invitation?

CHAPTER ELEVEN

Simplicity and Awakening in God

There is something very simple about God. Simple like a child's laughter that breaks forth, spontaneously, without guile. Simple like when you act, immediately and directly, to help someone who falls in front of you. Simple like the way you just find yourself awake in bed, all of a sudden, in the morning sunlight. God is simple like the way every moment of time, in its ordinariness, holds the gift of your life—like this moment, now.

Entering into a simple contemplative practice and remaining with its simplicity awakens you to God's simplicity. When you simplify your mind's actions in centering prayer, you reduce them from many to one. In contemplation, your many thoughts and strategies of finding truth, of seeking God, of discovering what your own life is about, are simplified into truth itself, into God, into life itself. In the clear, immediate, unadorned moment of life, God just is.

Life experienced in God reveals a naked clarity that shines forth through you. The contemplative person responds to the complexities of existence by simply awakening to God's ever-present life, as if rousing from a bad dream into the clear light of morning. Awakening in the ever-present life of God is the simplest thing you can do. Other actions generate complex strategies, convoluted machinations of effort. Awakening in God is simple.

From oneness in God comes freedom, life, creativity, insight, and the ability to love and serve more easily, without self-reflection or the intricate hidden agendas of the separate-self sense. From this oneness in God the rich diversity of life is born. Too often you seek this diversity, the things of life, on their own, apart from their source in God. The contemplative attitudes of simplicity and awakening shift you out of your complex struggles to find and hold onto the diversity of life on your own terms alone. Simplicity brings you into the true source of everything, that from which everything arises. As you live from the source of life, everything in life simply is, and it is simply yours. The richness of life is given to you out of contemplative simplicity. All you need do is to simply awaken to this truth, over and over again.

Don't Complicate This Prayer

When I was a young man, I lived for ten years in a small contemplative retreat community. For most of this time, my coleader, Mary Mrozowski, and I were the core of this small community. Others came for a while—one year, two years, three years—and practiced with us in residential training. We gave contemplative retreats for up to twenty-five people. Mary had raised a family, run her own small business, and was now a grandmother. She was also a deeply contemplative woman and something of a wisdom teacher for many of the retreatants.

Like the ammas and abbas, the Christian desert mothers and desert fathers who lived in the wildernesses of third- and fourth-century Egypt and Syria, Mary taught by listening to others and then offering succinct words of wisdom that came out of her centeredness in God. Her way of interacting was very straightforward and direct, arising out of the simplicity of the moment. Mary delivered these words of advice like pointed arrows shot at the center of another's confusion. If the other person was open and if a relationship of trust, rooted in God, existed between Mary and that person, the arrow would strike his heart, open his understanding, and help him on his contemplative path.

Once, on a weekend centering prayer retreat, as Mary was leading a group discussion, one of the retreatants said that when he sat down to do his centering prayer, he felt discouraged by how many thoughts he experienced. His sacred word didn't help. Could he make the sacred word longer, a sacred sentence he could chant?

Mary told him, "Don't complicate this prayer. Be simple with the word, and your prayer will become sacred." The man seemed surprised at her directness and quietly considered her advice.

In the next group session, the man said that during the centering prayer periods he had kept his word the same. But he still looked uncertain. Mary asked him, "What is the real problem?" He paused and then admitted that he was bored. His mind was restless. He didn't think centering prayer was for him; could he just think about Christ?

Mary said to him, "Let your mind awaken in Christ, and you will become sacred."

Again the man looked surprised. We had another period of centering prayer. In the next group dialogue, he reported what he had experienced. He said that at the beginning of that period, he found that he had just as many thoughts. And in the middle he did feel bored; his mind was very restless. Yet this time, he didn't think about his thoughts, and he didn't resist the boredom. He simply returned to his sacred word. By the end of the period, he found himself more settled, more at ease with having a simple sacred word, more comfortable with simply returning to it.

Over the years, this man returned many times to our retreat center. He became a committed contemplative. He practiced the contemplative attitude of simplicity in his centering prayer. As he matured in his practice, he learned the more receptive attitude of awakening in contemplation. Over time, his experiences of awakening in God affected his own actions in prayer more and more.

Simplicity in centering prayer and awakening in contemplation became less distinct in his practice.

This man was discouraged by the number of thoughts he was having during his contemplative practice. He wanted to make his sacred word longer, a sentence he could chant. Mary's direct advice to him was, "Don't complicate this prayer." By not complicating centering prayer, you root yourself in the foundation of simplicity. Mary said, "Be simple with the word, and your prayer will become sacred." In centering prayer, the attitude of simplicity begins to transform the word from any old thought into a sacred thought, a sacred word. Simplicity is the entry into the sacredness of contemplation. The attitude of simplicity helps contemplation infuse centering prayer practice. Complicating this form of prayer with other activities, other thoughts—even the thought of God—is fruitless.

The anonymous author of the fourteenth-century Christian spiritual classic *The Cloud of Unknowing* wrote, "Therefore I will leave on one side everything I can think, and choose for my own love that which I cannot think! Why? Because God may well be loved but not thought."[1]

Then the text gives its practice for choosing for love that which cannot be thought:

> A naked intention directed to God, and himself alone, is wholly sufficient. If you want this intention summed up in a word, to retain it more easily, take a short word, preferably of one syllable, to do so . . . And fix this word fast to your heart, so that it is always there come what may . . . So much so that if ever you are tempted to think what it is that you are seeking, this one word will be sufficient answer . . .[2]

In centering prayer the sacred word is meant to be short, simple, and singular. The technical term in Christian spirituality for this is *monologistic prayer:* the prayer of one (*mono*) word (*logos*). Along with its simple content, you simply return to the sacred word, without any other complications. As Isaiah says in scripture, "In returning and rest you shall be saved; in quietness and trust shall be your strength" (Isaiah 30:15).

You are saved from the manyness of your thoughts and the complexity of your mind by simple returning and resting. It is the simplicity of returning to the sacred word that brings your intentionality to life as consent, allowing your intellectual, reasoning mind to gradually awaken in the Mind of Christ.

God's Simplicity

The simpler you are in contemplative practice, the more you participate in God's nature. As Mary said to the man in the story, "Let your mind awaken in Christ, and you will become sacred." Grounded in the simplicity of God, you find you are much more than your scattered thoughts and emotions. You are created in the image and likeness of God. If you have been practicing the contemplative life for a while, consider your own experience of transformation. Your IQ doesn't necessarily improve. Rather, the transformation that contemplation initiates shows its fruits in life, as the Mind of Christ comes to life more and more in you, expressing itself in greater compassion and freedom. The fruits of God's life in you express themselves in a straightforward way, naturally, effortlessly, plainly, cleanly, without any added affectation or decoration. If you go to the dictionary, you will find that these adjectives are the synonyms for simplicity! Freedom is found in God's simplicity.

Meister Eckhart, the great medieval Christian contemplative, said that God is infinite in his simplicity and simple in his infinity.[3] Like the simple ground you stand on, the ground that sustains you all the time, God is always here. What do you have to do to find this ground? In the Christian contemplative tradition, you cannot find it by thinking about it. There is nothing complex about receiving the Mind of Christ. Begin by practicing the intention to let go of other thoughts and embrace the simple consent of unknowing faith. As this consent deepens, be transformed as you let go of thinking about your thoughts. And, ultimately, simply recognize the solid ground you are already standing on, right here and right now. The life of Christ is given, here and now. Just awaken in it, as you would wake up from a bad dream—the nightmarish illusion of being separate from God, from other people, and from all creation.

Jesus said, "Unless you change and become like little children, you will never enter the kingdom of heaven" (Matthew 18:3). Little children are, quite simply, simple in mind and being. Life is given without you having to earn it. You are in relationship with God at the level of your being. In this relationship, you don't have to do anything but just be in God. Just receive the divine life and love in which you are enfolded. Over time, as you commit yourself more and more to this love, any sense of yourself—false or true—disappears into the simplicity of God and the present moment itself. When you let this happen, everything becomes sacred, not because it is special, but because it is ordinary—precisely because it is not special! It is sacred because it simply is.

Awakening to a New Way of Cognition

The anonymous author of *The Cloud of Unknowing* wrote of two overlapping developments in prayer, using the image of two clouds to describe them. Being simple with returning to your sacred word helps open you to one "cloud," in which you forget about all other thoughts, without distinction, all thoughts of the whole "created world"—"in a word, everything must be hidden under this cloud of forgetting."[4]

In centering prayer, as you simply return to the sacred symbol and forget about every other thought, you open to the second, more important cloud referred to in the title of this classic book. As you commit to living in the cloud of forgetting with regard to thoughts and "creatures" (people, places, and things and your thoughts about them), you live in a second cloud in relationship to God, a cloud that is dark and obscure to the intellectual way of your mind's knowing:

> By darkness I mean a lack of knowing—just as anything
> that you do not know or may have forgotten may be said
> to be "dark" to you, for you cannot see it with your inward
> eye. For this reason it is called a "cloud," not of the sky
> of course, but "of unknowing," a cloud of unknowing be-
> tween you and your God.[5]

The first cloud has to do with your thoughts; the second cloud has to do with your thinking. As you are simple with your sacred word, you develop a new relationship with your thoughts in the cloud of forgetting; as you are simple with your restless, intellectual mind, you develop a new relationship with God in the cloud of unknowing. Awakening in the cloud of unknowing brings forth a new form of cognition that is aglow in a new and deeper form of faith—the living faith that apprehends God as a direct experience rather than a concept you think about. This is contemplation. You come to it not by complicated strategy, but by simply awakening, as if you were waking up from the nightmare of your separation from God. In the words of Jesus, "And what I say to you I say to all: Keep awake" (Mark 13:37).

The outlines of branches on a clear winter sky, the clean lines of a monastic cloister, the direct insight into reality that only later takes shape as a concept—all life is grounded in the simplicity of direct, unmediated knowing because God is the source of everything. To awaken to this deeper form of cognition, you must let contemplative simplicity deepen within you, in the Mind of Christ. The deepening of centering prayer into contemplation is a deepening of faith, the faith engendered by simply consenting to God. In scripture, Paul points toward this form of cognition and faith when he says, "be transformed by the renewing of your minds" (Romans 12:2).

Forgetting and unknowing are negative images that point toward the new cognition brought forth as centering prayer deepens into contemplation. Simplicity and renewing are positive images for the way of forgetting and unknowing.

It doesn't matter whether you prefer positive or negative images for contemplative practice and the transformation of faith. In centering prayer, when your intellectual mind is restless and bored, simply return to your sacred symbol amidst the restlessness. Let go of being dependent upon thoughts and the thinking process. Then God will transform the thinker behind the thoughts and the thinking process involved in the old way of cognition. Trust that a deeper level of your mind's activity is being renewed in you. Your thinking process is being transformed in the Mind of Christ. The divine presence acts in you as you journey through restlessness. With simplicity, restlessness becomes a doorway into the deeper transformation of contemplation. Don't get drawn into thinking about complex strategies during centering prayer. Remain simple and let yourself awaken in Christ, in contemplation.

Simplicity in Life

In contemplative practice, acting with the attitude of simplicity helps your mind simplify many thoughts into one thought, one intention—that of consent to God's presence and action. As your actions in practice become aligned with the gift of contemplation, you receive the simplicity of God. You gradually become a sacred word yourself, silently spoken by God to the world around you.

This dynamic is symbolized in the famous scriptural story of Jesus's encounter with the two sisters, Mary and Martha. Mary is sitting at the feet of Jesus, listening to him. Her sister, Martha, is consumed and distracted by the details and activity of preparing a meal for Jesus. Martha complains to Jesus about what her sister is doing, telling him to get Mary to help her in her distracted busyness. But Jesus answers, "Martha, Martha, you are worried and distracted by many things; there is need of only one thing. Mary has chosen the better part, which will not be taken away from her" (Luke 10:41–42).

Spiritual teachers throughout the centuries have pointed toward this story to illustrate the value of the contemplative life. Martha represents the active life and Mary the contemplative life. Mary's only action is listening to Jesus's words, simply attentive to his presence as the Word of God. Jesus says that this simple action is the one thing necessary—the better part of life, better than the distracted activity of Martha. He affirms the value of contemplative simplicity in Mary's prayerful stance.

But there is more to the story. Mary and Martha represent two valuable parts of your own nature. You are both contemplative and active. The greater spiritual task is to discover Mary's contemplative way of relating to Christ's indwelling presence and then integrate the simplicity of contemplative practice into active life. This includes integrating the divine presence with your active mind. You need to bring Mary's simplicity into Martha's activity, in both your interior and exterior lives. As Teresa of Avila said, "So be occupied in prayer not for the sake of enjoyment but so as to have the strength to serve. Mary and Martha must combine."[6]

Practicing the contemplative attitude of simplicity in prayer while experiencing complex thoughts and boredom helps you realize greater simplicity in active life. For me, this means being able to simply settle into the ordinary present moment at my desk when my computer is starting up. Rather than anxiously distracting myself with another activity, I better appreciate the ordinary moment in God and am more focused when the machine is ready. It means being present to another person in deeper listening attention, letting the Mind of Christ touch her heart beyond what I can do with my many words and great insights. It means acting from a more intuitive mind even while engaged in intellectual thought. It means greater acceptance of myself and other people when they or I make mistakes or do not show the fruits of prayer in life. The effects of prayer in life are fundamentally fruits of the simplicity of contemplation.

Contemplative simplicity in life means greater freedom and compassion—straightforward, natural, effortless—expressed as a fruit of God's simplicity acting through you. While simplicity is primarily a gift that comes as a fruit of centering prayer, you can also observe simplicity through your actions. The glimpses of inner simplicity that come as gifts can help you to live more simply. In a world of environmental crisis, consuming less is an expression of compassion for other people and all creatures. Driving the car less, eating more simply, and conserving energy are intentions and acts of prayer as valuable as reciting the Our Father. Practicing the contemplative attitude of simplicity helps you practice the adage "Live simply so that others may simply live." Awaken to the gift of God's life in you—the only thing that ultimately makes it possible for you to express the life of God, through yourself, in the world.

Reflective Exercise

Pause for a moment in silence and consider:
- How does being simple help your centering prayer deepen?
- How do you awaken to God in prayer?

CHAPTER TWELVE

Gentleness and Effortlessness

In contemplation there is a delicate balance between doing and being. You bring all of yourself to the contemplative path, including your actions, your efforts, and your dedication, yet action that becomes too effortful interferes with your receptivity to God. Too often effort is contaminated with struggle. Although human struggle itself can be discovered in God's grace, struggle that is oriented toward a goal separate from you excludes your deepest nature, discovered in God's eternal presence within, from the contemplative path.

Acting in gentleness shifts you out of the struggle to find God. Gentleness is necessary for the deepening of centering prayer. Your actions become more and more subtle in centering prayer as contemplation awakens in you. Actually, the sense that you have to achieve something, find some deeper depth, or go somewhere other than where you are now to discover God, is an illusion. Let contemplation come effortlessly to you, as a continual gift out of the gifting nature of God. Contemplation is effortless in the same way that the falling of snow is effortless. It is effortless in the same way that a light breeze blowing on your neck is effortless. It is effortless in the same way that the petals of a flower open into the sunlight. In receptive effortlessness, there is nowhere to go, nothing to deepen, not even any need to be gentle. The depth of contemplation is just being, effortlessly, in God.

Christ's life within you is gentleness itself. Contemplation involves letting Christ's gentle life become your own life. In contemplative practice, you gradually find that you are drawn into letting your effort burn away, letting it evaporate in the radiant light of God's gentleness. Let go of struggle. Let go of struggling against struggle. Easily and continually let go and relax into Christ's unseen, gentle nature within you.

As you ease into contemplation, you are enfolded by Christ's gentleness. As you go deeper, your actions become colored more and more by effortlessness and infused with greater receptivity. You live in grace, in God's nature, beyond any felt experience of struggling or even of being gentle. At this deep contemplative perspective, God's presence holds everything and excludes nothing, even your own effort. The mystery of God is gentle beyond even gentleness. In deep contemplation, the only response you can make is to just effortlessly be in the gift of God's inner life. Then you realize that God's inner life holds all of life. There is no effort in God; everything is already accomplished. As you approach union with God, you are drawn into greater effortlessness in contemplation.

As Christ's gentleness becomes the source of your prayer, gentleness comes through you, both in prayer and in action. In life you gradually learn to move through the busyness of your ordinary world with greater ease of spirit. As you struggle less in life, divine love and compassion act through you, arising spontaneously and easily as an expression of God's presence within. In contemplative gentleness, you learn to act more and more in line with God's life and action. As you consent to God's presence and action, you find that everything, including your own actions, arises from God's gentleness. God's presence acts in you and through you.

Gentleness is at the heart of centering prayer. During the first years of teaching of centering prayer in the early 1980s, we instructed people to "gently return to the sacred word." Then, after a few years of experience teaching centering prayer, the language of the basic instructions was modified to say "ever so gently return to the sacred word." In those first years, we saw how important it was to stress gentleness. The addition of the phrase "ever so" highlighted the attitude that most of us need to hear again and again: that we act in contemplative practice with gentleness—great gentleness. Practicing centering prayer with gentleness opens you to the effortlessness of contemplation, which in turn helps you be more gentle in returning to your sacred word.

A Homeward-Turning Love

John Ruusbroec, the extraordinary contemplative of the Middle Ages, had a wonderful phrase for the kind of action into which we are invited with contemplative practice. He said that we realize our union with God through grace and a *homeward-turning love*.[1]

A homeward-turning love—such a rich image. Have you ever been on a journey far from home? When you are traveling on roads far from home, you need to know exactly where and when to turn your car. With actions that are alert and focused, you need to follow directions and signs. Without some effort, you will get lost. But what happens when you get close to home? You don't have to make the same kind of effort. You don't need MapQuest or even a GPS. When you are traveling close to home, a part of you remembers the way without having to plan, without having to make efforts, without trying to get anywhere. You turn the car naturally and easily, and all of a sudden you are in the driveway. You are home.

Such is the way with contemplation. God, our true home, is everywhere and ever-present. In the effortlessness of contemplation, you just say yes to the gift of this presence. Contemplation is simply consenting, simply receiving, simply being, in God, in a gentle, homeward-turning love.

Ever so gently returning to the sacred symbol in the practice of centering prayer provides a ground for contemplation's effortless, natural homeward turning. In a sense, the effortlessness of contemplation is easy, yet it is something you seem to have to learn and relearn over time—a long time. So it helps to remember that this homeward-turning movement is one of love, rather than self-initiated effort. Let the deepest part of yourself, created in God's image of love, effortlessly take you home.

Let Go of Your "Struggle Word"

When I see someone concerned, frustrated, and tense about contemplative practice, I often remind that person of the value of relaxing in prayer. Once, a student of mine who had been doing centering prayer for a while was uncomfortable in his prayer and thought that if he changed his sacred word he might have an easier time. I suggested to him that he didn't have a sacred word but a "struggle word." That idea helped him to laugh and relax a little bit. I invited him to be gentler with his word instead of changing it, and he was able to return to his word with less frustration.

It is easy to try too much in centering prayer. When you do, your sacred word becomes a struggle word. Physical symptoms of trying too hard include tension and headache; psychological symptoms include impatience and frustration; spiritual symptoms include despair and searching beyond the moment of what is already given to you, already here, in God. Tension, frustration, and despair come into prayer as you search and yearn for something you already have—or, rather, Someone who already has you.

You try so hard to be gentle. Then you try not to try. You struggle against struggling. Futility comes and perhaps a sense of being trapped in your own isolating self-effort. Your struggles may be especially frustrating after you have learned that acting with gentleness helps your contemplative practice deepen. You may feel hopeless. You may experience this situation as a beginner; you may also experience it as a longtime practitioner. What can you do when even gently trying to be gentle doesn't work so well?

God's nature is already in you. God's love is gratuitous, unearned. There is no effort to receiving this love, no struggle to awakening in this nature. Just easily, gently say yes to it, as a gift already given, already here. That is the essence of contemplative practice. That is what you can do to open to the gift of contemplation. You just practice, acting in gentleness, until you experience how God's gentleness is awakening in you. Then receiving the gift of contemplation is effortless. Then you can live in it, effortlessly, more and more. With time, gentleness and effortlessness intertwine in your actions in centering prayer and in your receptivity in contemplation.

"Come to Me, All You That Are Weary and Are Carrying Heavy Burdens"

As you move deeper in contemplative practice, you learn how to yield to Christ. Christ's nature itself is gentleness. Jesus said, "Come to me, all you that are weary and are carrying heavy burdens, and I will give you rest. Take my yoke upon you, and learn from me; for I am gentle and humble in heart, and you will find rest for your souls. For my yoke is easy, and my burden is light" (Matthew 11:28–30).

The movement from a practice such as centering prayer to the greater gift of contemplation is a movement from your action of gently returning to the sacred symbol to the more profound action of effortlessly receiving Christ's gentle presence as the true source of your prayer. As you lay down your weariness, your heavy burden, and your effort and learn from God, you realize the true nature of the divine life. In contemplation you realize Christ as the true source, the agent, the actor, in your prayer and in your life. In prayer, you disidentify from effort and from the separate-self sense as you yield to the gift of Christ's presence within and discover your true identity and true freedom in God.

As you yield more and more to God in prayer, Christ's gentleness actually becomes the source of your practice. Dualistic struggle disappears. You no longer find yourself trying to find God. Even more, you no longer are in a dualistic relationship with God.

God's Effortless Nature Acts in You

In contemplation, the sacred symbol and Christ are not the objects of your practice. As contemplation effortlessly comes forth, Christ is the subject in you who is awakening to his source—the Father, the Abba—in the effortless, imperceptible movement of the Spirit. In contemplation, the inner life of the Trinity—Father, Son, and Spirit—comes alive in you, awakening from an unconscious ontological reality hidden within you to a conscious experience that gradually becomes the reality of your meditation, your life, and your service of others.

The movement of the Spirit between the Father and the Son is imperceptible because there is ultimately no distance, no separation between the two. As Jesus said, "The Father and I are one" (John 10:30).

There is no dualism in the Trinity, no effort to get anywhere in the inner life of God. The Trinity is eternal, so it does not operate in linear time, where separation, distance, and struggle rule the day. In contemplation you rest in effortless, open awareness as this Trinitarian life breaks into time and envelops all your dualistic struggling. All futile efforts to find truth dissolve into the eternal present life of God.

Effortlessness is a very subtle action that you learn in contemplation. You learn it because it is part of God's nature in you. As contemplation comes alive within, God's effortless nature acts in you. So in the receptive contemplative attitude of effortlessness, what you do and what God is doing in you are aligned, brought together in love.

The presence of God is continually acting in you, but very gently. God is gentle beyond any perception you can have of gentleness. All you need do is awaken to the presence of God acting in you as the ground of your being. With time, you learn to practice effortlessly, without holding onto or resisting any object of awareness; any memory of the past or concern about the future; any thought, feeling, sensation, image, or perception, even of God. Awaken in grace to the ever-present gift of the infused Trinitarian life of God. In the contemplative attitudes of gentleness and effortlessness, there is a natural deepening of your contemplative practice; ever so gently returning to your sacred symbol, your separate sense of self yields to Christ's gentle presence. Then this presence awakens to its source, his Abba, in the Spirit—a subtle experience of God relating to God in you, rather than the dualistic action of you trying to find God.

Preserving Gentleness in the Midst of Life, in Joy, and in Suffering

How does it look when the contemplative attitudes of gentleness and effortlessness begin to surface in life? Some might think it looks like acting one way: mild and tranquil. It could.

But transformation in Christ does not create one image of holiness. The Spirit does not destroy human uniqueness. Allowing the contemplative attitudes to surface in life does not necessarily mean speaking softly or moving slowly. Gentleness and effortless-ness are interior attitudes that show themselves as different external behaviors in different people.

Mary Mrozowski, the spiritual mother of the retreat community in which I lived, was a dynamo of activity, a bustling whirlwind of action. I often heard her coming home from one of her extended teaching trips, her high heels banging down the hallway. Yet for me she was an icon of contemplative gentleness because she rarely got caught in inner struggle. Mary held activity in inner trust, through her contemplative practice. One time when we were leading a retreat, Mary was making lasagna for twenty-five people. As she got ready to heat up the lasagna before lunchtime, she discovered that the ovens weren't working. I got a little bit concerned, but when I looked at Mary she didn't seem concerned and seemed to be taking a moment of prayer. Then she phoned next door to our neighbors, bustled the lasagna trays over there, and brought back the piping-hot lasagna before serving it just fifteen minutes late. She said later that she did have a feeling of anxiety, but rather than getting caught in it and struggling to find some solution on her own, she turned to God. Her practice of responding with gentleness during contemplative practice allowed God to create some inner spaciousness, so that she could pray for a moment in activity and more easily discover a practical solution to a potentially frustrating problem. Mary's interior contemplative gentleness expressed her growing union with God. As Francis de Sales said, "The one who can preserve gentleness in the midst of sorrows and sufferings and peace in the midst of the multiplicity and busyness of affairs—that person is almost perfect."[2]

If someone living in the attitude of gentleness is almost perfect, what is perfection? Because the idea of perfection in our society often engenders paralyzing self-judgment, effort, and struggle, I suggest that perfection includes being gentle with your imperfections. Imperfections, in prayer and in life, are a gift, for they keep you human and dependent upon God. My friend Mary was not perfect; she sometimes forgot about her spiritual practice. Like everyone else, she was sometimes irascible and difficult to live with.

But trusting in the love of God, gently offering your imperfections, your humanity, to God brings you into greater effortlessness. God comes through your transparent humility, to others and to yourself.

As gentleness comes alive in your prayer, God's life, love, and compassion come forth in your actions. As gentleness comes alive in your actions, God's life comes into the world through you, simply and unobtrusively. God's life is not just a transcendent presence at the ground of your being; God's life includes a dynamic action of love that emerges out of this transcendent divine presence into the immanence of human life. You are meant to share the life of God, given to you in prayer, with the world, in your actions but most of all in your presence. When you are faithful to contemplative practice, the kingdom of God that is within and among you births forth into life. The kingdom is built in the world around you, as your simple acts of serving others become more and more effortless expressions of the divine life.

Reflective Exercise

Pause for a moment in silence and consider:
- How has gentleness helped your centering prayer deepen?
- How can you be effortless in prayer?
- What is another attitude, image, or phrase that describes gentleness and effortlessness in the deepening of your centering prayer and your contemplative life?

CHAPTER THIRTEEN

Letting Go and Letting Be

Letting go is at the heart of centering prayer. As you let go, you open into God, unfold toward others, expand into life. Letting go frees you from the tight grip of self, from the trap of obsessive mind, from the contraction of self-will. Practicing the active attitude of letting go establishes you on the contemplative path. As contemplation comes alive within you, learning the more receptive attitude of letting be allows the divine life to gradually become your life. As you practice deep trust and let everything be, just as it is, in God, you participate more and more in the divine life itself. As centering prayer deepens, letting go yields to letting be—being in God's Being. As you taste more and more what it is like to let everything be, just as it is, in God, you can let go more easily. And over time, letting go and letting be are commingled in your contemplative practice; there is little distinction between what you are doing and the way God is being in you.

Effort and discipline have their place in the spiritual life. The contemplative attitude of letting go is *active*—an action you take. Continuously letting go of your attachment to thoughts, emotions, and all things in order to recognize God as the source of thoughts, emotions, and all things requires intentional, repeated actions. But at some point, your own effort yields to God's presence and action; this yielding comes when you practice the *receptive* contemplative attitude of letting be. Letting be is a more refined movement of faith and trust that, in the words of Julian of Norwich, "all shall be well, and all shall be well, and all manner of things shall be well." Everything has its fulfillment, in God. As you practice the attitude of letting go, you disidentify with thoughts and open to a new sense of who God is, a new level of freedom, a new sense of yourself. The attitude of letting be brings this new sense of God, this new freedom, this new sense of who you are, to life in you.

Contemplation happens within like a stone easily falling out of your hand when you simply open it, like rain descending earthward out of a full, dark cloud. Like gravity, God's life is an unseen energy of which you become aware when you let go and let be.

The contemplative attitudes of letting go and letting be open you to God's nature, which is love. Love frees you from attachment, transforms self-will into willingness, refines your own efforts to let go into Christ's gentle surrender within you. God's love invites your surrender. Surrendering to love is not defeat. It is liberation. Letting go arouses surrender in you; letting be opens you to surrendering your surrender. You are a vessel of God's compassion in the world as God lets go into life through you.

The Monkey Who Won't Let Go

If your sacred word is *let go,* your inner dialogue when you sit down for centering prayer might sound like this: "I'm introducing my sacred word . . . Let go, let go, let go . . . Wonder when my car will be ready at the shop. Let go, let go, let . . . Sound system's great. Let go, let go, let go . . . Dad's test results . . . back today . . . Let go, let go, let go . . . let go . . . Don't know what to do if he weren't here . . . Let go, who would I be without him? . . . Aghh! Oh these thoughts! How can I let them go? . . . Is prayer going to be a washout today? Ah, can't get free! What to do . . . Can't let go

. . . No good at this . . . What was my sacred word anyway? Oh, let go, Let go, let go . . . let go . . . *let go,* let . . . go . . ."

One of the first things you learn in any contemplative practice is that you can't think yourself into letting go. Hanging on to the idea of letting go is not letting go. In contemplative practice, letting go means not paying attention to the content of your thoughts and instead ever so gently returning to God. Centering prayer gives you a sacred symbol for this returning, to help establish this essential attitude in the beginning of your contemplative practice and to reinforce your discipline, surrender, and detachment as you continue on the spiritual journey.

Of course, as you sit down in centering prayer, you immediately become more aware of the thoughts that are in your mind. You also become more aware of the things in your life to which you are attached—favorite possessions, the people you love, your own sense of self—the things in life that fill your thoughts and stimulate your emotions. In faith you may realize that the things of life are mere expressions of God in the world—that, in the traditional language of Christian spirituality, "creatures" are rooted in their unseen, secret source. Even if you cultivate a relationship with God, the unseen Creator of everything that is, creatures still stimulate thoughts and emotions. This is understandable. Without God, the good things in life easily hold you. Gerald May says that "Saint Augustine once said . . . God is always trying to give good things to us, but our hands are too full to receive them . . ."[1] You are attached to thoughts to the extent that you are attached to things in life. Hence, learning to let go of thoughts in centering prayer by consenting to God teaches you how to let go of attachment to things in life by consenting to God.

The English word *attachment* comes from the old French word *atachier,* which means "to be nailed to." Actually, thoughts are not an obstacle in contemplation—only the thoughts to which you are nailed, the thoughts that linger in your mind and hold you to them. A well-known metaphor told in meditation circles describes this bondage. In certain areas of Africa, tribesmen hunt monkeys with a very simple yet effective trap. The hunters cut a small hole in the shell of a coconut, scoop out the insides, insert a sweetmeat into the hole, and leave the coconut on the floor of the jungle. A monkey smells the delicate sweetmeat, finds the coconut, and puts its hand in the hole to retrieve the bait. But once it has grasped the bait, the monkey's clenched fist is too large to be pulled out through the hole. The coconut is too heavy for the monkey to carry very far. If the monkey would just let go of the bait, it could get its hand out! The trap is perfect because the monkey will not let go. It is captive, a perfect ingredient for monkey soup.

Like the monkey, you get trapped when you grasp your thoughts. Something in you believes that your survival is bound to these thoughts. You don't know how to let thoughts go. You cannot let go, directly, on your own. Trying to let go of thoughts just binds you more tightly to them. You cannot let go of thoughts through self-will. There is no way you can directly do it. You need the indirection of an intermediary. In centering prayer, you have a sacred symbol that expresses your consent to God. Practicing with the sacred symbol brings a greater ability to let go, for in your consent to God, another aspect of your own being is accessed in you, from which you can let go of thoughts more easily.

Often, you see how full your hands are by how full your mind is—full of thoughts that hold you. Learning to let go in contemplative practice frees you from this bondage. In centering prayer, you just return to the sacred symbol and let God within you let go of the thoughts that hold you.

As you are freed, in God, of attachment to thoughts, you have a freer relationship with everything in life. You become freer to love the things of life in God and let them go in God. Being in

a living relationship with the Creator, the source of life, brings you into the right relationship with these creatures, the things and people of life that arise out of this hidden source. John of the Cross said that we have more "joy in creatures" through "*dispossessing* them"—letting them go. This kind of freedom lets love flow more easily to others through you.

Floating in God

Contemplation is a lot like floating. You might use a life preserver to learn to float in a pool. You hold onto the life preserver, then you let go of the poolside wall. Your legs lift off the bottom. You move around, still making contact with the walls of the pool, but able to let go; you don't have to hold onto the walls as you did before. You feel supported, while at the same time you are getting a sense of what the water is like. You feel the water's buoyancy. As you use the life preserver in this way, you begin to trust more in the unseen qualities of the water. You let yourself be in the water. The pool walls are there, but they do not hold you anymore. Something else does. You are floating.

This is what contemplative practice is like: you let go of the thoughts and emotions that are like walls limiting you, and you learn to let be, as if you were floating in God. In centering prayer, your sacred symbol is like a life preserver that helps you let go of thoughts, enabling you to move into the deeper waters of life with God. As contemplation comes to life in you, you learn how to let all thoughts just be, by returning very easily to your sacred symbol or not returning to the manifest form of the symbol at all.

As centering prayer deepens into contemplation, you use the sacred symbol the way someone who is learning to float uses a life preserver. You introduce the sacred symbol and return to it when engaged with other thoughts. But as you progress, you also learn

how to lightly return to the sacred symbol, barely touching it in your mind. You go further when you learn how to let it go to test the waters of the prayer. Then you let it go completely when you are ready to rest in the indwelling spirit of God.

In the depths of contemplation, you just let all things be, in the Beingness of God. In God's Being, all thoughts and emotions rise and fall on their own. Letting all thoughts be is a very receptive and mature contemplative attitude. Your growing trust in just being in the waters of the Spirit allows you to let go of even the thing that brought you there. In the depths of contemplation, holding onto a symbol, no matter how sacred, is preserving the wrong life—a life of form. Holding onto a sacred symbol keeps you in the active attitude of letting go when really you are being drawn into the more receptive attitude of letting be.

You may wonder, how do you let go of the sacred symbol? You can't try to let it go. You just let it be in your mind, let it refine itself so that the sacred word becomes a sacred whisper, the sacred breath just breathes in you, the sacred glance becomes a subtle seeing within, the sacred nothingness is everything, everywhere. Then God lets the symbol go in you. Your attitude of letting be lets God let go in you. Your actions become aligned with God's action in you. The delicacy of contemplative practice is in learning to sense when God is letting the sacred symbol go in you. Then you cooperate with the deeper inner movement by letting it be and letting it go. Learning in contemplative practice is subtle and experiential, like learning to float. You cannot really describe how to float, just as you cannot really describe how to pray contemplatively. Contemplation and floating have to be experienced to be understood and have to be practiced to be learned. However, knowing and practicing the contemplative attitudes of letting go and letting be help you recognize how your own direct experience is teaching you.

Letting Be

Although letting go of your sacred symbol is not emphasized so much in the basic guidelines of centering prayer, in the deepening levels of contemplative practice you are always invited to let the sacred symbol go and let all things be. Thomas Keating says:

> In the beginning it is hard to hang on to your intention without continually returning to the sacred word. But this does not mean that you have to keep repeating it. . . . In centering prayer, the use of the sacred word is designed to foster the receptive attitude. The interior movement toward God without any word is often enough.[2]

The attitude that quickens this interior movement of receptivity is letting be.

If you hold onto the sacred symbol, repeating it all the time, you may temporarily feel that you are doing your contemplative practice correctly. But holding onto the sacred symbol all the time like a life preserver safeguards the wrong life; it doesn't allow contemplation to come alive in your experience. You may feel you are being faithful to God, but contemplation is beyond forms and symbols, even sacred ones. As the Psalms say, "For God alone my soul waits in silence" (Psalm 62:1). The sacred symbol is only a sign of your consent to God. You need to let it go to consent to God alone. You only return to the sacred symbol when you need it, when you are engaged with your thoughts.

What are God's presence and action like? Imagine right now that you are floating in a calm, peaceful, warm ocean. You hear the seagulls calling. The afternoon sky above is spacious and clear. You have let go of your concerns, your efforts, and are just floating. In the water, the boundaries of your body feel indistinct. You begin to merge with that which is around you, feeling safely enveloped in the water. You feel like you are in a womb, at one with a presence that supports and nurtures you. There is nowhere to go, nothing to do except to be in the gift and gifting of this ever-present enfolding love.

Just be. Just let the thoughts and emotions in your mind be, like ripples or waves in the water that pass by when you don't try to do anything with them. There is nowhere to go in contemplation except into the mystery of Christ. In this mystery, a new sense of yourself comes alive—one that no longer exists on its own, but is found, continuously, in an ongoing relationship with God. Letting be is the skillful response to the action of God, your partner in the prayer, for it is God who draws you deeper into the contemplative attitudes.

Who really lets go in the depths of contemplative prayer? God and the deepest part of you. God comes alive in your prayer, as a result of deepening practice and the utter giftedness of love. As Christ lives more and more in you, letting go becomes an attitude that is infused into more and more of your prayer life.

God Is Love

At one point, the scriptures speak very clearly about the nature of God. In his first letter, John writes, simply, "God is love." The kind of love that is God is not a sentiment or emotion, but is the being, the source of life itself. John goes on to write, "God is love and those who abide in love abide in God, and God abides in them" (1 John 4:16).

Contemplation is the realization of God as love—love that you might feel on a sensory or emotional level, but that, more importantly, exists as the ground of being itself. You do not feel this love, but awaken to it. The unseen presence that supports you, the love that enfolds you in prayer, is God. In contemplation, God's presence as love settles your efforts, draws you into trusting, guides you into being able to let go and let be. Letting go of the sacred symbol to float in and become one with God's presence is actually an act of love—a love that brings you into relationship with God's unseen mystery in contemplation. Although you might sometimes feel or sense it, this is not a kind of love that depends upon emotions or felt experiences. The contemplative attitudes of letting go and letting be are essentially acts of *being* love rather than acts of *feeling* love. That is why this kind of love is a gift, for it is the gift of God's Being. Letting go in contemplation is an act of love that is drawn forth by God's presence—by love itself.

In the deepening of centering prayer, as you continue letting go, you lose your own limited, surface sense of self and conditioning by self-will. As Jesus said, "For those who want to save their life will lose it, and those who lose their life for my sake will find it" (Matthew 16:25). Jesus's life was a life of love, a life of letting go and letting be.

Blessed Are Those Who Mourn

The contemplative attitudes, including letting go and letting be, are naturally expressed in life. Letting go and letting be in life mean letting God become the source of every moment, every relationship, and every activity. The love that is God is expressed in letting go.

A friend of mine lost her job in the recession. She told me that even though her centering prayer practice gave her faith and perspective that she would find a new job, she was still surprised at how much this change in her life upset her. During her ten years at her position, she had developed close friendships, enjoyed her work, and had no desire to change jobs. Her friends who didn't understand the contemplative path told her not to be concerned, it was just a job, and she should get out there looking for a new one as soon as possible. But recognizing how sad she felt, she didn't start looking for another job right away. She shed genuine tears. She also felt angry. It was only after two weeks of transition that she could even think of looking for new work.

But, gradually, she did. She said she felt her job search was less frantic because she had taken time to let go and find God in it. When she did find new work, she was able to open herself to it, fully, having taken time to mourn the loss of her past life. After four months at this new job, she told me how happy she was with the change. She better understood what Jesus meant when he said, "Blessed are those who mourn, for they will be comforted" (Matthew 5:4).

God as love lets you love more, so it is understandable that God in you would invite you to mourn the loss of something you love—even a job. Once you have allowed yourself to grieve, you are free to move into new life again. Change, loss, and death are part of life.

The contemplative attitude of letting go may come alive consciously sometimes as an acceptance, even a happiness, that you are not in control, because there is Someone greater who is. You may experience a subtle shift of belief, as trust comes a bit more into your life. But, primarily, the fruits of contemplative practice are hidden, expressed as an unknowing immersion in the present moment *without* the concern, the effort, or the machinations of the separate-self sense. The inner transformation brought about by contemplative prayer awakens you into the moment of life in God without your thinking about it, without your holding consciously onto your thoughts, the people, and activities of your life, your needs, your beliefs, your tears. Thoughts, people, and tears arise in you now as an expression of God's life. When Jesus says, "Blessed are those who mourn, for they will be comforted," he releases you from the need to mourn in any particular way. The Beatitudes express in a theological way the life of Christ in you, coming alive in subtle ways as a fruition of your prayer life.

You move into the deeper fullness of contemplative prayer and the contemplative life when you learn to let go and let be. You learn to float in God in prayer in order to swim with God in life. Faithful to God working through your commitment to practice and to life, you are drawn into the deeper waters of contemplation.

Reflective Exercise

Pause for a moment in silence and consider:

- What kinds of thoughts are the hardest for you to let go of?
- How do you let go of your sacred word?

CHAPTER FOURTEEN

Resting and Being

In the sixth century, Gregory the Great defined contemplation as resting in God. Resting in God does not necessarily include the felt sense of physical relaxation. It is not so much about feeling emotionally peaceful or even necessarily having a quiet mind. Contemplation can include bodily relaxation, emotional peace, and a quiet mind. But contemplation is much more. Contemplative resting is a resting of your being in the Being of God. With this very subtle resting, your mind, heart, and bodily awareness can also rest and just be in the source from which thoughts, emotions, and sensations arise: God's indwelling presence. Through contemplation you gradually learn a new freedom; you discover a new peace, a peace that passes all understanding and serves you by giving you a ground, a center in the busyness of life.

The active contemplative attitude of resting—just letting go and resting in God's presence without any effort, without any action to change your experience—opens you to contemplation. Contemplation is like falling asleep at night. You don't learn to fall asleep; you don't take classes or retreats on how to fall asleep. It's something natural that happens in you, when you let it. The more you strive to get to sleep, the more you can't rest. If you let go of trying and let an inner presence of relaxation come, amidst your tiredness, and then you yield to that inner presence, the next thing you know you will be waking up in the morning light.

The contemplative attitude of resting is an action like yielding to the inner presence of relaxation when falling asleep. It is something you do, but it is a very subtle doing. Retreats and classes on contemplative practice are more about helping you recognize how you naturally rest in God rather than showing you a fail-safe strategy for achieving God's peace. The subtle presence of God helps bring forth the contemplative attitude of resting just as the sense of physical relaxation in bed brings forth sleep.

However, in contemplation, felt experiences of God's presence are not a goal, but a gift that, like a compass, orients you on the spiritual path into God's Being. God's Being is a greater reality than God's presence. While resting in God's presence is an extremely important contemplative attitude to practice, being in God's Being is even more valuable.

Being is a more refined, more receptive attitude that balances and brings the active attitude of *resting* to fruition. Being means not doing anything other than just being. In a sense, the attitude of being is an undoing. You let go even of trying to rest. In the attitude of being, there is no presence of God to find or yield to. God's Being just is. Whatever is there, activity or rest, just be in it, for activity and rest are both held in God's Being. Your receptive attitude of being and God's Being become one. Action and presence are one.

In the depths of God's Being, rest beyond resting. Wait beyond waiting. Be beyond being. With time, you learn how resting in God helps you be in God. You experience how being in God's Being helps you learn how to practice resting in God's presence.

Restlessness in the Desert

When I was a young man, I traveled with my old car packed full of my belongings westward across the United States in search of a spiritual community and teacher. As I drove down from the Rocky

Mountains into the high desert of Utah, something unexpected and unplanned happened.

I had never been in the desert, and something about it captured me. There was a palpable, still presence there. I slowed down, turned off the highway, drove down back roads, and parked the car. In a moment I found myself resting my gaze in the desert emptiness. The city consciousness I had carried with me across country began to yield to something else. I found my mind settling into it, like a child laying his head on a soft pillow.

That night I changed my plans, and I stayed and camped in the desert. The next day I took extra time on my journey and explored the area. I wandered along the canyon rims. Having grown up in the Michigan suburbs, surrounded by woods, lakes, and fields, to me the desert was a completely foreign landscape. It seemed a hard place in which to exist. As I hiked and looked around on that second day, I found no human or animal life. All I could see was vast, empty sky and a horizon devoid of trees and vegetation. The desert felt like a barren void. I was initially intrigued. After a while, my mind became unsettled, restless.

That second day in the desert my mind was very busy. The still presence of the previous day was gone. The desert became like a mirror reflecting my inner restlessness. Thoughts flew around everywhere in that empty sky. I felt anxious. My agitation grew. I felt that if I didn't get out of there, I might explode—or implode.

But in that thunderous desert silence, I also somehow sensed a quiet invitation to remain. I sat down. I noticed my breathing, how it felt to simply breathe. As I exhaled, the tension eased. My mind was still racing, but I felt something within me settle into just being there, no longer seeking anything different.

Then I noticed tiny blooming flowers around me. As I let go of trying to fill up the desert, let go of trying to escape it, I began to perceive subtle life and beauty in it. The sand was patterned and contoured, sloping down and around to a canyon that met the sky in a brilliant blue seam. I found a different kind of peacefulness in the desert when I didn't struggle or move against it. My mind just was. My desert restlessness of mind became radiant when I just let it be.

After a few days in Utah, I continued westward on my spiritual search. Yet I had found something in the desert. Or I had been found by something there, something that later showed its face as a mysterious Someone. The desert became my teacher. Its emptiness invited me into just resting—resting in its being.

Resting in God

Contemplative resting is not so much experiencing God as an object of consciousness—an image, concept, or thought—but a resting in God as the source of all images, concepts, and thoughts in consciousness. Receiving this kind of rest means learning both how to let go of inner restlessness and also how to listen, recognize, and yield to the increasingly subtle awareness of God's presence within.

The early Christian contemplative teachers of the third and fourth centuries, known as the desert mothers and desert fathers, spoke of *acedia,* an inner dryness, restlessness, emptiness, and boredom that you can experience in the contemplative life. The sayings of the desert mothers and desert fathers included Christianity's first written teaching about contemplative practice: how to handle acedia and thoughts in prayer and how to follow the path into union with Christ.

The desert mothers and desert fathers lived in the desert because they found it a place where they could become aware of God's presence, a place where God's action could transform them. They advised their students to simply remain in the emptiness, to wait through the inner restlessness or listlessness that they called acedia. As my experience in the desert of Utah shows, when you practice the contemplative attitude of resting, the restless thoughts, feelings, and images settle and release into their source: God. As it says in the psalms, "Be still before God and wait patiently . . . Be still and know that I am God" (Psalm 37:7, 46:10).

The Being of God

With practice, contemplative resting unfolds into relaxing into being—God's Being. You may ask, *what is God's Being?* In scripture, God was revealed to Moses on Mount Horeb in the form of a bush that burned but was not consumed. Imagine this sight: flames breaking forth from dry branches that should be burned up in moments. But the branches are not incinerated, and time collapses as the branches and leaves remain. The bush was not destroyed; it just was, engulfed in flaming light, radiant energy.

Moses asked what name he should call God, and the voice from the bush said, "I AM WHO I AM . . . This is my name forever, and this is my title for all generations" (Exodus 3:14–15). *I am who I am*—a statement of ineffability, of transcendence infused into existence, a name of being. God says, "I just am—existence, unending, unconsumed." This image and these words point to an experience in which linear time collapses into the radiant present moment of God's Being. Eternity is held in God's Being. How do you apprehend God's Being? Just be.

Jesus manifested this mystery of "I-am-ness," of Beingness, in human form. In John's Gospel, when Jesus was asked who he was, he said, "Before Abraham was, I am" (John 8:58). Jesus, the Logos, who was with the "I am" of God in the beginning (John 1:2), came into the manifest world of time and activity two thousand years ago. Christ's resurrected presence is always here, always in you as the hidden ground of your own being. Let the manifestation of I-am-ness, Christ's resurrected presence, lead you into his more secret source, the I am who I am. Trust in being; beneath and between and beyond all efforts and strivings and mistakes is the eternal ground of God's Being, imaged in your own being.

The Attitude of Being

There is no way to find God's Being because it is already here. But by just being, you assume the attitude necessary to realize Being. Resting in God has a quality of dualistic effort to it; you as a subject are resting in the awareness of an object: God's presence. In resting there is still separation between you and God, a split between the activity of your mind and God. On my second day in the desert, just being with all that was, including the noisy, restless activity of my mind, allowed me to realize God's Being, I am who I am. There is no dualism to being in God's Being. Brother David Steindl-Rast quotes Thomas Merton as saying to him:

> The desert becomes a paradise when it is accepted as desert. The desert can never be anything but a desert if we are trying to escape it. But once we fully accept it in union with the passion of Christ, it becomes a paradise . . . This breakthrough into what you already have is only accomplished through the complete acceptance of the cross.[1]

The cross was Christ's way to his resurrection and the availability of his Being, his I-am-ness, for all time. The cross symbolizes the death of the separate-self sense.

The receptive contemplative attitude of being is also a death—that of separation and effort and struggling into oneness with the eternal now of God's nature, which is graced and gifted in a love that is ever-present because love is the nature of God. It is extremely hard to just be in God's love, for the separate-self sense wants to do something to achieve or perform or produce it. But we can't. Achievement, performance, and production have to burn away in the receptive contemplative attitude of being.

Just remain in meditation. Just sit there until future striving and past regrets dissolve into the present kingdom. Your sitting and God's ground conjoin in your realization of their oneness. Let stillness and movement be. Be in silence and in noise. Just be with spaciousness and contraction. Practicing the attitude of being during contemplation is taking God's stance, and God's stance is the eternal ground that holds and accepts everything.

Of course, it is hard to just be in such receptivity. That is why resting is the active attitude that accompanies being. Resting is something you can practice, something you can do, so that God's Being comes to life within to teach you what it is to just be. When you allow yourself to rest in God, spiritual presence comes to you. Then you have a middle ground for realizing God's Being. Then love that comes from deep acceptance awakens as the source of your own presence to others.

Resting and Being in Life

Sarah, a longtime spiritual friend of mine, has always had a profound commitment to the attitudes of contemplative resting and being. When I first met her, she was living as something of a hermit in the city. She took in graduate students' manuscripts that needed typing, working quietly in her apartment around her schedule of prayer and contemplative practice. She used to joke that her sofa was the place where she just sat with God, unraveling the workings of her mind and learning to just be. She was basically content with that orientation. Yet she wondered if, at some time, there would be some kind of work that she would do, writing perhaps.

After many years like this, God changed her world. Sarah met a visiting professor and found that, as she opened to the relationship, loving him was not separate from loving Christ. After a while, she moved to his home country overseas, and they married.

Her external life had a different flavor as she lived as a foreigner, learned a new language to navigate the basics of life, became a wife and, later, a mother. She was very busy. She had little time for solitude, but still did her contemplative practice after the busy world quieted down, late at night. Resting and being in God remained for her the ground that made her human life in the world possible.

Sarah found that her long training in solitude gave her a solid foundation for living such an active life. She still craved more solitude than she had, but she fully embraced her new life. Yet, as time went on, she also wondered if she would ever use her unique talents and gifts in writing or teaching about spirituality. As it was, her contemplative life was completely obscure, hidden from the world. Her family and a few friends knew she meditated, but I was the only one who knew about the depths of her contemplative practice.

After fifteen years, during which our only contact was exchanging periodic letters, I began to see her again when she returned regularly to the States. These visits were wonderful for both of us. On one visit, as we were traveling together to a center at which I regularly gave classes, Sarah again expressed to me her questions about writing. She felt that maybe her choice in life to get married years ago had prevented her from practicing enough and bringing the fruits of her contemplative practice to others in service.

When we arrived at the center, I introduced her to some of the participants as an old friend and contemplative practitioner. As I was preparing for the class, I noticed her having a lively exchange with one woman who also came to see me sometimes for spiritual direction. I knew from spiritual direction that this woman was struggling in a spiritual dark night and feeling depressed emotionally. I saw now how deeply present and attentive Sarah was to her, yet at the same time very animated and interactive. In that brief encounter, I noticed my directee lighting up, smiling, and coming to life in a way I had not seen for a long time. Their exchange lasted about five minutes. I taught the class and then drove Sarah to see her family across the state.

When I saw my directee a couple of weeks later in spiritual direction, she talked about how her spiritual darkness had lightened. In the time since Sarah's visit, my directee had been able to follow her centering prayer practice more easily and settle into a new sense of God. Her feelings of sadness and depression also lifted. She thanked me so much for that class I gave. Something that day shifted, she said, but she couldn't be sure what happened.

Nor could I. God works through us in hidden, mysterious ways. I couldn't say with any certainty, but I wondered if Sarah's long and deep commitment to resting and being in God had borne fruit in a simple and brief exchange with my directee. Perhaps Sarah's practice of just being amidst her seeking, doubt, and unknowing had created an open receptivity in her that God could use to touch another person who was trapped in seeking, doubt, and unknowing. Certainly my spiritual directee in her dark night needed precisely what Sarah embodied: God's Being.

Thomas Merton wrote of the contemplative desert:

> If you dare to penetrate your own silence and dare to advance without fear into the solitude of your own heart, and risk the sharing of that solitude with the lonely other who seeks God through you and with you, then you will truly recover the light and the capacity to understand what is beyond words . . . it is the intimate union in the depths of your own heart, of God's spirit and your own secret inmost self, so that you and He are in all truth One Spirit.[2]

The contemplative attitudes of resting and being in God have profound value in your own meditation, in the hidden ways this practice affects your life and the lives of others. Resting and being in God turn you toward a mystery that is beyond linear time—a mystery that is eternal because it is here, fully, now, in this and every moment. Resting and being transform the sense you have of how the world is made and how your actions and your meditation affect the world. The contemplative attitudes of resting and being turn you inside out to truth, in hidden ways that are only realized in the unknowing of the eternal moment of God's Being, in which there is no separation from anyone or anything. When doubt, concern, and a desire for achievement arise in you, above all, trust—be—in God's Being.

Reflective Exercise

Pause for a moment in silence and consider:

- What are you striving for and how might this striving be affecting your centering prayer?
- How does the attitude of being help your contemplative practice?

CHAPTER FIFTEEN

Embracing and Being Embraced

During the time when I lived at the retreat community, there was one occasion when we were in our midday period of silent meditation. A few guests were with us. I was leading the session, which included keeping time for our half-hour period of centering prayer and ringing the bell at its end. In the middle of the period, I heard one of our guests across the room rustling in her seat. Over the next minutes, she fidgeted back and forth, sighing heavily, adjusting and readjusting her posture. Attending to the environment in the room was my responsibility, so out of concern for her and the others, I opened my eyes to see what was going on. She looked very uncomfortable. Then all of a sudden she got up and, with a determined and angry look on her face, strode silently across the room toward me. She veered toward the bell at my right side. She reached down, grabbed the striker with a firm embrace, and with a grand movement, swung it. The bell sounded. She let the striker go, turned around, and silently left the meditation room.

Sometimes challenges and suffering arise in centering prayer. Learning how to embrace God in the challenges and how to be embraced by God in the suffering are essential for persevering on the contemplative path. I later met with the woman who had sounded the bell in our midday meditation session, and she and I explored these contemplative ways of embracing.

Important challenges on the contemplative path include *resistance, dread,* and *the dark night.* This chapter looks into these three challenges and how you can respond to them by embracing and being embraced by God in them. I've included a story from my own life that I hope illustrates how to respond to these challenges.

Resisting Self-Knowledge

The obsessive thoughts, the waves of emotion, the storms of spiritual suffering that can come during centering prayer and contemplative practice are sometimes overwhelming. You may want to do anything to flee from them—even impulsively aborting your commitment to practice, like the woman I described in the meditation room did. These situations are challenging because while they are happening, God seems like a fairy tale. Resistance and other psychological defenses, such as repression, denial, and projection, come up, keeping you from encountering the pain of the human condition.

Unfortunately, these defenses also keep you from God. In the Christian tradition, the experience of the raw, existential depths of the human condition—in all its felt separation from God—is called *self-knowledge.* Contemplative practice not only brings you into contact with this kind of self-knowledge, but also helps you avoid getting trapped there. You have to go through self-knowledge to come to the abiding knowledge of God. Skillful contemplative practice—the kind our bell-ringing retreatant and I explored after she aborted her meditation session—embraces God in obsessive thinking, in emotions, and in spiritual suffering. After learning how to embrace God in suffering, she was able to sit through her practice with greater faithfulness and more commitment. Skillful contemplative practice helps you relate to resistance and self-knowledge.

Anger, fear, sadness—from the deep perspective of faith, God is in these "afflictive" emotions, acting through them to open you to your humanity. When you are open to your humanity, you can better show compassion to others. Compassion literally means "to suffer with." Compassion means relating to others with your shared humanity, which includes your challenges, your suffering, and your feelings. Joy, happiness, pleasure—God is in these "positive" emotions, moving through them to bring you to fullness of life, as you are freed from attachment to them. Boredom, ennui, dryness—God is in these "neutral" emotions, moving through them to help you appreciate the wonder of ordinary life.

By resisting emotions, you also resist the transforming action of God. Resisting self-knowledge holds God's presence at arm's length.

A Deep Embrace

Embracing is the opposite of resisting. Embracing is an active contemplative attitude that helps you shift into a deep perspective of faith. The transformative process in centering prayer is likened to a divine therapy. In this process, emotional wounds from your past are brought to light in the healing relationship with God. Intense emotions, such as anger, fear, and sadness, that arise in times of practice, often without any connection to your current life, are a part of the Spirit's healing and transforming action. They are being brought to consciousness so you can be freed from them, and—even more importantly—freed in them. Being *freed in* feelings means being able to experience them as part of your humanity without being trapped in them, without being identified with them, without letting them escalate into emotional states from which destructive behaviors come. *Feelings* are a gift, a part of human experience to be embraced. More complex *emotions* and *emotional states,* colored by guilt, shame, attachment, and addiction, arise from resistance and the buried trauma that conditions the psychological aspect of the separate-self sense.

For example, anxiety is a natural and adaptive feeling when you are walking close to the edge of a cliff. In this situation, anxiety alerts you to danger. But when anxiety develops into fear and panic, you can become paralyzed. In traumatic situations, when your safety is threatened and you have no way to effectively fight or flee from the situation, emotions such as panic become trapped in your psyche and in your body. The buried trauma affects your life like a hidden emotional program. Trauma comes from emotionally dangerous events like abuse, loss, or neglect, as well as physically dangerous situations. But there are ways to gradually release trauma and learn how to find more freedom in real-life situations as you discover a different relationship with your feelings.[1] As you heal from past trauma, it is possible to learn from feelings like anxiety, rather than resisting them; when you resist them, they easily build into more complex emotions like panic. Once you learn to let go of emotional programs conditioned from past wounds like abuse, loss, or neglect, then healthy relationships in the present are more possible.

Skillful contemplative practice helps transform your relationship with feelings because it decreases resistance. As resistance to feelings is decreased, you open to what in the Christian contemplative tradition is traditionally called *purification*. The separate-self sense is purified by contemplative practice. Emotional trauma and emotional programming from the past trap you in needs for esteem, control, and security, creating a false sense of self. This false self and the unconscious psychological barriers within, held in place by resistance, are the psychological side to the separate-self sense. The therapeutic response on our part in the divine therapy is to feel the feelings associated with the transformation, in relationship with God. In light of the loving relationship with God, the emotional programs of the unconscious are "unloaded" into conscious awareness. The opportunity of trusting God and embracing the Spirit in emotions, especially emotions that arise during purification, is a skillful response that can be practiced in centering prayer.

Your relationship with God, developed through ever more subtle contemplative practice, is what makes the healing and transformation of the divine therapy possible. When unconscious emotional programs are unloaded during centering prayer, continuing to return to the sacred word can actually stymie the ways the Spirit is transforming you and your feelings. Feelings are embraced through felt awareness, not thought. Thomas Keating has a suggestion for these situations:

> One way to deal with intense restlessness, physical pain, or emotions such as fear or anxiety that may arise at such times of unloading is to rest in the painful feeling for a minute or two and allow the pain itself to be your prayer word. In other words, one of the best ways of letting go of an emotion is simply to feel it. Painful emotions, even some physical pains, tend to disintegrate when fully accepted.[2]

To get a sense of what embracing feelings is like in meditation, think of the way you accept or embrace another person. In an embrace, you not only touch another person; in a real embrace, you enfold the other person with both arms. You draw the other person to yourself. You hold that person to your heart; you feel that person's being, bringing it close to you. A deep embrace is actually an expression of oneness in a relationship. If the relationship has pain or brokenness in it, you may have to work through avoidance and resistance in the embrace. You may need to begin by simply touching hands before trying to go further. To really embrace another, trust needs to be built, and rebuilt, in the relationship. If resistance is strong, it may take time and practice to move into a deep embrace.

On the contemplative path, embracing is valuable because you are *embracing God in the feeling,* not embracing the feeling alone. This embrace is meant to be attentional rather than intellectual. With your attention, you *feel* the energy within the feeling or sensation. Returning to the sacred word can engender effort because you can easily relate to this sacred symbol in your intellectual mind, as a thought. Thinking about the feeling leads you away from it, into resistance. Rather, it is as if, in being confronted with a feeling, you open your arms wide enough to embrace the Spirit through, with, and in the pain. God envelops the pain—and you. You may need to gently touch just a corner of the pain in order to build trust in God. In time, you hold God and the pain to your heart, so to speak. In doing so, you are changed, opened to being transformed in the mystery of God's embrace of you, in your humanity. Rather than resisting who you are, you become a little more human. In Christian contemplative practice, the way to being fully human is through embracing the divine presence and action in all things, including emotions.

Dread

It is not just emotions and feelings that are purified as a result of contemplative practice. Purification works on different levels and includes transformation of the deeper structures of consciousness where the separate-self sense lives. Simply speaking, union with God comes as the separate-self sense gradually lessens. As you begin to consciously recognize your union with God, you can experience something that, classically, is called *dread* in the Christian tradition. Contemplative dread is the feeling-state that comes as the separate-self sense is purified. Dread often includes feelings such as diffuse anxiety, along with a deeper sense of emptiness or void, because the separate-self sense underneath the emotion is being purified. The fullness of God is experienced as emptiness by the separate self; resistance to the emptiness arises, and feelings such as anxiety surface to consciousness.

Here is how Gregory the Great, early in the Christian tradition, described what dread is like for an advancing contemplative practitioner:

> Then it happens that the enlightened mind entertains the greater fear, as it more clearly sees by how much it is at variance with the rule of truth . . . Though the mind may have conceived but a distant idea about God, nonetheless, in considering his greatness she recoils with dread and is filled with greater awe because she feels herself unequal even to the traces of contemplation of him.[3]

The light and love of God illuminate the separate-self sense, and it feels its distance from God. Dread includes a vague or sometimes a strong anxiety on the surface of consciousness because the underlying separate-self sense is being transformed as union with God deepens. This death of the separate-self sense is a wonderful development in your relationship with God. The question is, what can you do during times of dread?

In order to transform dread, be with the emptiness behind the feelings; discover that God is in the emptiness. Learn to rest in the emptiness behind the surface feelings associated with dread. Discover that emptiness is full of God. Because the separate-self sense has to fall away into the emptiness, patient practice during dread is important. Your trust in God needs to deepen. Remember, God's subtle presence in the emptiness of the separate-self sense is coming to life in you. With patient and trusting practice, at some point you will experience how God's presence embraces you in emptiness. Become one with this embrace. A new sense of you comes alive, a you that is interconnected with, not separate from, all that exists, *in the emptiness.*

Before you can be embraced by God in the emptiness of dread, you have to have a solid foundation established in meditation. This solid foundation includes embracing the Spirit in feelings. If trauma surfaces from the past, it may be valuable to seek support.[4] With a solid foundation of meditation practice and support, you can open to God's embrace of you in the emptiness of dread; as the separate-self sense dies, you experience true freedom in God, and can love others more freely.

Death and Life

A few years ago, my stepmother telephoned me and told me she had been diagnosed with brain cancer. She had married my father when I was thirteen. Her vivacious spirit brought life into our family, and my siblings and I grew to see her as our mother. After hearing the news of her illness and offering her support, I prepared for contemplation, offering prayers for her, especially that she experience God's presence during her illness. As I began centering prayer by introducing my sacred symbol, immediately I noticed anxiety within. As thoughts of my stepmother's illness came and the anxiety grew into fear, I remembered my training in meditation. I let go of returning to my sacred symbol and began embracing God in the fear. After a while, the anxiety passed, replaced by waves of sadness. As I embraced God in the sadness, waves of love for my stepmother washed over me. Thoughts of concern for her came and went, but I had the presence of mind to continue being present to God by embracing my feelings for her.

As my meditation continued and I embraced the Spirit in the feelings of love, I experienced a more diffuse anxiety. It was unsettling because it arose with a sense of unnerving desolation, a raw emptiness. A few stray thoughts of my birth mother's illness, suffering, and death almost forty years earlier passed through my mind. I knew that purification was going deeper, through my emotions around this event and into the way my sense of self had been constructed around the trauma of early loss. The unloading of the buried emotions was exposing the structure of the separate-self sense. I recognized this situation as dread. I continued embracing God in the emotions and began resting in the emptiness. After my period of meditation ended, I started making plans to travel to be with my stepmother during her surgery.

Over the next months, as I traveled back and forth to see her, much of my contemplative practice, in centering prayer and in activity, was about being attentive to my experience and embracing God in the waves of feelings as they continued washing over me, colored by memories of my birth mother's suffering and death. The deeper emptiness of dread also came and went as I experienced the dissipation of part of my separate-self sense, which was built around the emotional programs of loss and unresolved grief. During some of my time in meditation, I rested in open awareness in the inner emptiness; at other times, I found myself caught in resistance. When I could, I remembered God's compassion and practiced embracing the feelings and sensations associated with the resistance itself: bodily tension, constriction, and tightness.

A few months after her surgery, complications developed with my stepmother's recovery. Her condition worsened. My sister called me to say that Mom was coming home, in hospice care. Before her surgery, she had made a living will, courageously allowing herself only the simplest medical procedures and pain medication for her end-of-life care. I flew to her home to be with her, my sister, and my brothers.

My stepmother was unconscious most of the next days and nights. Sometimes she moved through a semiconscious state, tossing about in her hospice bed, mumbling and processing memories of her life. Once in a while, she woke up and spoke a few words to us. She was not taking any food and very little water.

Not wanting my stepmother to be alone, I stayed up at night with her, doing contemplative practice for her. I saw how, as she processed memories from her early life, she was also opening more to God. I sat on the floor by her bed, praying for her, embracing God in the feelings present to me, and resting in the empty depths of the night. My meditation practice was my offering to her.

After a couple of days, we noticed that the more she slept, the more conscious moments she later had. After a good night's sleep, on the fourth day, she sat up in bed and talked coherently with us for ten minutes. We wondered if she was rallying. Perhaps she even had a chance of recovering!

During my vigil later that night, though the lights were off, I noticed my stepmother was awake again. I wondered if she were able to drink water. I gave her a little liquid, but she soon began tossing and turning. I heaved a sigh of despair. I wanted her to live. If she could only stay asleep for the rest of the night, she might be better tomorrow.

I remembered my practice and embraced God in my exhaustion, my grief, and my love. My stepmother tossed and turned, mumbling words and memories about her life. Out of my tiredness, I sternly told her, "Mom, now stop talking. You've got to get some sleep!"

She did stop. After half a minute, I heard her voice clearly: "Give me a break." Her humor was still alive and well.

I was stung. I felt that by trying to control the situation, I had lost my presence. Longtime contemplative that I was, I had lost my composure, my ability to be present to her at this most important time. I said, "I'm sorry, Mom. I just want you to rest." With a sense of humility, I surrendered to God.

There was silence in the room. Then she said, "We're doing all right here." I saw her in the moonlight, her tongue moving in thirst. I swabbed her dry lips. There was nothing else I could do for her. I surrendered. In the darkness of the night, God was present.

She went back to processing her memories, and I returned to my silent, exhausted vigil. But something in my vigil was changed. God remained, not a tangible presence I could describe or feel, but a presence in emptiness. Amidst my stepmother's cries and my tiredness, I felt embraced by the mystery of Christ's own death and resurrection.

The next day she was exhausted. Her breathing was slowing. The family gathered at her bedside. All of a sudden her eyes opened. She looked at us. She saw us on her deathwatch. Fear passed across her eyes. She pushed herself up a bit and said, "I've got to get out of here."

I heard myself saying out loud, "Mom, you're home. We are all here. You're safe. We love you." She stopped, looked around, then closed her eyes and relaxed back down in bed. She was asleep in an instant.

She had another day in this life, with a few rare moments of consciousness. After she died, we gathered around the bed and said goodbye. I applauded her, thanked her, and wished her well.

And I offered a prayer of gratitude to God. The simple words that had come through me when she sat up in bed the day before were the ones she most needed to hear: she was home, we were with her, she was safe, and loved. These words were spoken in my own voice. But I knew they came from Christ's embrace of her, and of me, in my sense of failure and brokenness at being able to care for her. She was cared for, alive, in God.

Her dying process was an incredible witness to me of her spiritual journey into God, accelerated at the end of her life. During her life, she had not consciously embarked on the contemplative path. She had her own way of being spiritual. I clearly saw how, approaching death, she drew, and was drawn, closer by God. As one of her witnesses during those last days, I had no time for quiet, solitary prayer. But in my vigil, in the darkness of the night, I embraced and was embraced by God. The pain of my grief was touched by the mystery of God. The emptiness of my dread became fully transparent to God. Out of that clear light, words of comfort were spoken.

God's Embrace

As contemplation deepens, your own practice of embracing God in suffering yields to being embraced by God. Transformation includes dying to the separate-self sense, experiencing now, in this life, the mystery of death and resurrection. For someone following the Christian contemplative path, Christ's embrace of suffering and death is the mystery that embraces you when your own efforts come to an end. Your own practice of embracing God in suffering is done in the light of God's divine embrace of the human condition. In the light of God's embrace, the human condition, in its isolation and despair and emptiness, is transformed.

Christ experienced the depths of the human condition. When he was all alone praying in the Garden of Gethsemane, he knew he was about to experience extreme physical suffering; he was going to be crucified and die. Imagine for a moment the human emotions that passed through him. When scripture (Luke 22:44) says that he sweated blood, it only hints at what his inner experience might have been. To me, his eventual response expressed his own "practice," his human experience, and his self-gift to God, his divine source: "Father, if you are willing, remove this cup from me; yet not my will but yours be done" (Luke 22:42).

I have counseled many contemplative practitioners in spiritual direction. I find that, at some point, everyone confronts the mystery of suffering and death, physically, emotionally, and spiritually. The thing that sustains a Christian practitioner encountering challenges and suffering on the contemplative path is surrendering, *in emptiness,* to Christ's embrace, to the gift of God's presence transforming suffering and death. Thomas Keating says, "Seeing the presence of Christ in the present moment is the way to transformation . . . Just say, 'Here he comes! I embrace him—hidden in this trial, in this dreadful person, in this stomach ache, in this overwhelming joy.'"[5]

The Dark Night

The dying of the separate-self sense is sometimes very poignant. The emptiness of this death can be tinged not only by emotions, but also by a sense of failure, despair, and, especially, the loss of God and those things that have been your essential spiritual supports. God as an object outside of you falls away just as your own sense of self as a subject who apprehends God dies. You experience a taste of the experience behind Jesus's words on the cross, before his death: "My God, my God, why have you forsaken me?" (Mark 15:34).

In these periods, called *dark nights,* God is actually present in the suffering you experience, but in a subtle, less dualistic way. At these times, God is also acting in the absolute death of your sense of who you are, the death of what your life is about, even of who God is for you. Those things that have been essential spiritual supports are falling away outside of you, so a new way of being can arise in you.

The image of the dark night is very rich. Centuries ago, when John of the Cross first wrote about the dark night, there was no electricity. At dusk, there were no city lights. The disappearance of the sun left a real emptiness, almost a blindness, in which movement was difficult and most activities had to be curtailed. The darkness that came in John's Spanish evening was complete. The light and life of day were over.

Likewise, in a contemplative dark night, your life changes. Meaningful spiritual activities—prayer, devotion, practice, service, relationship to your tradition—no longer seem to have the same effects. Instead of oneness with God, the separate-self sense reappears. In the dark night you may even feel the effects and the sense of self even more strongly. Your path becomes even more unknown and unknowable. You may feel more vulnerable to "demons"; your old fears resurface, and depression may set in. If you have given your life to Christ and the contemplative path, the disappearance of God's light genuinely feels like despair, or even death.

John of the Cross does speak of an eventual dawn, but he also lauds the dark night itself. Transformation is in the night. When out in the country, have you ever settled into the twilight experience? What happens to your sight? Your eyes slowly begin to adjust to the darkness. After a while, you begin to see in a new way. You begin to develop night vision. With night vision, you can see by the subtle light of the stars, a light that was always there, even during the day. During the daytime, the sun overwhelms the stars, so you never know there is another light possible—until night comes. With night, a whole new universe opens up above you, subtle, brilliant, and beautiful. This new world grows as long as you let it, as long as you avoid turning on an artificial light. You receive the gift of a new kind of transforming vision in the night.

How do you develop night vision on the contemplative path, in the midst of challenges, suffering, and death? You develop night vision by *embracing God in the suffering and being embraced by God.* You are transformed in the dark night when you practice both the active attitude of embracing the felt sense of suffering, in sensations and feelings, and the receptive attitude of allowing yourself to receive the embrace of Christ. This dual practice of the active and receptive attitudes works on two levels: the surface level of your conscious experience and the deep level of your separate-self sense. John of the Cross speaks of two kinds of dark nights: the *dark night of sense* and the *dark night of spirit.* Transforming the purification that comes in the night of sense means to sense, feel, and experience, in faith, that God is present and acting in your human experience, especially now, in the most difficult emotions. Transforming the purification of the night of spirit means that you receive the spiritual embrace of Christ's passion when you are plagued by such inner demons as temptation, destruction, and ignorance, which arise in despair, doubt, and self-contraction. The sense and spiritual purification intermingle. Each type of purification has its own challenges.

Some modern contemplative writers also speak of a third dark night: the *dark night of self.* In the dark night of spirit, God disappears. In the dark night of self, "self disappears—or gradually diminishes until it is finally gone,"[6] as you are subsumed in the embrace of the inner life of the Trinity itself, when you lose any fixed point of self-subjectivity in the subjectivity of what is called the Godhead.

Whatever contemplative dark night you are confronted with, the task during spiritual darkness is to avoid getting caught in yearning for the light of day. Don't bother searching for the old ways God's presence touched you and woke you up from the dream world of the separate-self sense. The task is not to search for an artificial light. Transformation in the night is all about moving to a more subtle level of perception. Dualism dies in the darkness. The contemplative task is to remain in the darkness itself until it becomes radiant in your embracing of God and in God's embracing of you.

The contemplative path also humanizes us. Humility is the fruit of the process of becoming more human before God. We cannot truly serve others in a sustained way without humility. Becoming ever more human—opening to God's mercy and extending God's compassion to our own weaknesses—grounds our love for others in humility. The way to becoming divine includes becoming more human, in all our giftedness and uniqueness, in all our brokenness and dependence upon God. This is not an abstract teaching.

The need to change your relationship with your own experience of being a human being becomes evident when you sit through a few sessions of contemplative practice. You confront your own neurotic mind, your own wild emotions, your own broken heart. Find God in these and in all things. Then you can find all things in God.

Reflective Exercise

Pause for a moment in silence and consider:
- How have you practiced the attitude of embracing?
- What was a time when you have been embraced by God?

CHAPTER SIXTEEN

Integrating in Life and Emerging in God

Prayer and activity often seem separate. Moments of inner peace appear distant from the busyness of outer life. The contemplative path easily feels different from life in "the world." But these felt separations can be lessened and even resolved by skillful contemplative practice. In fact, more skillful contemplative practice is based on integrating those things that appear separate spiritually, like prayer and activity.

Your view of God also affects your centering prayer practice and contemplative realization. When you see God as a thing, an object outside of you, then you are always seeking to draw closer to something separate from you. It is as if you were a fish, looking for life-giving water in distant drops of rain that are confined to a realm far above, which you can never reach. Likewise, when God is an object, your spiritual journey will always be colored by separation. Even the view that God is inside you, although true and valuable, locates God in a place. Seeing God in a place tends toward objectification and even stimulates goal-seeking in meditation.

The deepest contemplative intuition is that God, rather than being located in any one place, is a dynamic mystery in which life is always emerging. Imagine what would happen if the fish realized that life-giving water is not only above it as raindrops. What if the fish discovered that water makes up most of its body and, even more importantly, that it lives and moves and has its being in an ocean of water, all the time? What if your view of God expanded as much as the fish's view of water? With an expanded view of God, your contemplative practice could include sensing waves and currents in life and thus realizing that you are in an ocean of divinity. It is the movement of waters of the Spirit that awakens you to the mystery of the life you are always in. The subtlest form of contemplative practice is not about relating to a thing, but about realizing that you are always in God's dynamic, encompassing life—a life that is emerging all around you. God is more like water than merely like rain. God is beyond you, within you, and you are in God.

Integrating and emerging are the final contemplative attitudes that not only complete the other dispositions, but also crown them all in a greater unity. By integrating those things that seem separate spiritually and practicing according to God's continuous emergence in life, you orient yourself to unity.

Separation

On our regular Sunday afternoon hike, an old friend of mine, Jim, was planning a retreat. He needed a break from his busy and stressful life building affordable houses for low-income families and caring, with his wife, for a foster child with special needs. Jim had practiced contemplation for twenty-five years and had been on many retreats. Rather than going to a monastery, this time he was planning on camping in the desert for a week. As he told me of his plans, I heard in his voice a deep yearning for silence and solitude.

I saw Jim a week after his return from the desert. On our hike, he spoke about what had happened on his camping retreat. The first few days were wonderfully peaceful as he found the inner and outer rest he needed. Then, on the afternoon of the fourth day, he was meditating on a huge rock overlooking the desert canyonlands.

As God's inner peace flowed into him, he found himself suddenly standing up and exclaiming, "I've had enough of peace! I don't care if I ever have it again." It was such a strong intuition that he jumped off the rock and strode away from his peaceful site. All of a sudden, the idea of seeking God's peace was repugnant. His remaining desert days were spent wrestling with two experiences: resting in God's peace and being dissatisfied with peace.

My ears perked up as he told his story. I thought, "How wonderful! Jim is on the edge of a great contemplative breakthrough!" You might wonder, how could that be? Resting in God and experiencing inner peace are important. Jim's life was very stressful and busy, and he needed some tranquility. How can you have enough of peace when your world is so active, especially after you've given yourself to the spiritual journey for so long? What breakthrough was Jim near?

Integrating Peace and Busyness

It is understandable that Jim needed some inner peace and freedom in order to follow the contemplative path amidst the activity and challenges of ordinary life. Sometimes freedom from inner turmoil and suffering is the fuel that motivates you on the spiritual journey. Yet one of Jim's recurrent problems in his practice was his attachment to God's peace, his search for transcendence. In his search for God's divine Truth, Jim was not seeing the ways the human truths evident right before him were also in God. His marriage, his job, his family life were not separate from his contemplative path. The joys and sufferings of ordinary life, even busyness, are part of the spiritual journey. In order to discover the greatest insight of the Christian contemplative path—that the divine and human are inseparable both in Christ's Incarnation and in your own life—you have to let go of the search for transcendent peace. In seeking so hard, Jim was missing the greater truth that was right before his eyes, immanent in his ordinary life.

At some point, the contemplative path naturally develops so that God starts regularly breaking forth in the guise of ordinary life. After many years, Jim's journey had reached this natural threshold, a doorway into a new life of unity in God that is the fruition of contemplation. I saw that Jim was on the threshold of this realization of unity not because I am an expert at accomplishing it myself, but because I am convinced of my need to practice it! Why not orient your own journey toward this perspective from the beginning by consciously integrating those things that seem separate in your contemplative life, like prayer and activity? Then you experience the fruition of the path along the path itself.

You integrate things that seem separate by practicing on both interior and exterior levels. One place to practice integration on an interior level is in centering prayer. When you see thoughts as being an "integral, inevitable, and normal" part of the process of the prayer, you accept thoughts and open more easily to the healing and purification process.[1] When you let go of seeking peace in prayer, you find peace integrating more easily in your life. When you practice ways of integrating prayer and activity, you affirm that peace is not an end in itself but a means to something greater. Teresa of Avila clearly puts inner peace in perspective when she says, "How forgetful this soul, in which the Lord dwells in so particular a way, should be of its own rest."[2] My friend Jim's exclamation "I've had enough of peace!" was a passionate way of expressing that he was forgetful of rest.

The attitudes you hold in the spiritual life, consciously and unconsciously, color your view, influence your expectations, and shape your choices. When you actively practice with the perspective that the effects of centering prayer are found in daily life, not in the period of practice itself or in any peaceful experience, you are practicing the attitude of integrating. Changing your attitude is the beginning of integration. Yet integration goes beyond changing your attitude, for integration involves actions, things you do to combine, merge, blend, and intermingle prayer and activity, inner peace and outer busyness—everything that appears separate. How do you practice integration in your own spiritual life?

You put the attitude of integrating into practice when you take time at the end of the period of your centering prayer to let go of returning to your sacred symbol, allowing yourself to reengage with your thoughts, feelings, and sensations as a way of integrating your spiritual nature with your human nature. You integrate prayer and activity when, at the end of your sitting practice, you pray for someone else or engage in another form of spiritual practice as an expression of the prayer in secret. There are specific ways of fostering these attitudes in centering prayer, some of which are mentioned in Chapter 2. These practices are the actions that concretely express the change in perspective that Jim had on his desert retreat.

Practicing integration helps unify in you the split between prayer and life, the separation between peace and thoughts, the dualism between inner and outer, the rupture between the divine and the human. When you let go of seeking one side of the interior dualism—inner peace, for instance—then its apparent opposite is found in God, too. The exterior split between prayer and life can be integrated in God. This is what Jim discovered as he perched on the rock above those desert canyons. His change in attitude came after a long time of practice in which he was seeking God's peaceful presence at the expense of God's action in life. The human, in all its busyness, messiness, and richness, cannot be left out of the journey into the divine for long.

God's Dynamic Life

A central assumption of this book is that you develop a more skill-ful contemplative practice as your own experience and view of God unfold in subtler and less dualistic ways. Progressing on the path of centering prayer deepens your experience of God, and vice versa.

This is what happened for Jim. I find it valuable myself to periodically examine my attitudes about God. Because dualistic ideas of spirituality are conditioned in us by experience, some theology, and even the term "God," let's explore some ideas and metaphors that point toward the contemplative intuition of unity and foster the attitude that your prayer and life themselves are emerging in God.

To give an example of the contemplative intuition of unity, Thomas Keating writes, "The four Gospels contain Jesus' program for revolutionizing our understanding of the Ultimate Reality and hence of ourselves and other people, and indeed of all created reality. This is the God that is manifesting who he is at every moment, in and through us and through all creation."[3] Some modern theologies, in line with this deep contemplative insight into unity, emphasize that God not only created the world in the big bang, but that creation is an ongoing process. Creation is continually happening materially and in less visible ways. Creation and the evolution of life are in God.[4]

God is more than a transcendent being watching over the world. God is active in life and is the dynamic reality in which all life exists. Centuries ago, Hildegard of Bingen said of the Christ, the Word of God, "The Word is living, being, spirit, all verdant greening, all creativity. This Word manifests itself in every creature."[5] The deeper you go into contemplative practice, the subtler and more dynamic God becomes. Ideas of God are turned on their heads by your deepening encounter with the living God through contemplative practice. Let the flip side of this realization happen. Let your contemplative practice be opened toward the unity of prayer and life by a vast, dynamic, unitive attitude toward God. As your experience of God deepens, you also experience the interconnectedness of all life. Father Laurence Freeman says, "Understanding the meaning of unity accompanies faith at the personal level of growth in relationship to ourselves and to others. But it also manifests at the social and global levels as we endure the crisis of our time and the divisions and conflicts that it produces."[6] The intuition of unity unites us with every other living being. Unity challenges us to build a more just and equitable society based upon the interconnection of all life.

God's life comes to consciousness in you in the deepening of contemplation. You see more from God's point of view—from the inside out rather than from the outside in. The contemplative path brings you first from seeing God as a thought of yours to the experience that God is beyond thoughts, then to the greater mystery of realizing yourself as a thought in the mind, being, and emergent life of God. Can you sense the shift in perspective from an objectified God to an emergent God of unity?

God is an eternal, unseen ground sustaining everything in life at every moment. Even more, God is the mystery in which life emerges. Scripture says, "In him we live and move and have our being" (Acts 17:28). Notice the subtle view of God revealed here. This piece of scripture is not just saying that God is within you as the ground of being beyond passing thoughts. This intuition is not just implying that God is in ordinary life. It says that all of human experience and life, inner and outer, is *in God*. And even more, in saying that "we live and move and have our being" in God, this part of scripture goes to the heart of unity. God is an emerging mystery; prayer and life are not separate from this emerging.

In the Middle Ages, John Ruusbroec spoke of this dynamic view of our emerging in God in this way: "The Spirit of God breathes us out from himself that we may love and do good works; and again he draws us into himself, that we may rest in fruition."[7] God is not in any one place. God is not any one thing. God is like breathing, and you and I are living and moving and having our being within that breathing. Resting and peace are needed. Let your rest and your peace be more than stagnant goals. Love, good works, and activity are needed. Let the activities of your life be more than duties, done so that you can get back to your meditation spot. Let rest and activity both be found within a greater unifying, effulgent mystery: God.

Because of God's indwelling in you and your indwelling in God, the deepest Christian contemplative intuition into God's revelation—the unity of the Spirit in the Trinity—is what awakens you to God's dynamic life. When you find yourself emerging in God, in the unity of the Spirit, you have a completely new perspective on everything that looks separate.

Emerging in Prayer

Once, I was hiking in the high mountains and came across a small lake. I could see that there was no water emptying into this lake, and I wondered how the lake was being fed. It was only when I dove in for a swim that I discovered the secret of this lake's existence. As I swam to the center of the lake, I felt movement underneath me. Water was gently surging upward from the lake bottom. Sensing the flow of water with my feet, I realized that the source of the lake was an underground spring. The only way to discover the unseen source was by immersing myself in the lake, becoming one with the water and experiencing the water's movement—just like a fish!

Likewise, the way to realize God's unity is to immerse yourself in the life of God and discover its movement, both in your prayer and in your activity. The life of God is Trinitarian. The Spirit is the animating energy in the Trinity, moving between the Father and the Son. Realizing the Trinity through the emergent movement of the Spirit is the way into the prayer of unity. This approach is not about praying *to* the Spirit. This approach is not about praying *in* the Spirit. The prayer of unity involves a non-dual realization of the Trinity itself, in which inner life and outer life are inseparable. The entry into this realization of the Trinity is the Spirit, rather than the Son or the Father.

At the conclusion of his most mature work, *The Spiritual Canticle,* John of the Cross hints at what awakening to unity is like when he speaks abut the *movement,* the *breathing,* the *emerging* of the Spirit of the Trinity:

> By His divine breath-like spiration, the Holy Spirit elevates the soul sublimely and informs her and makes her capable of breathing in God the same spiration of love that the Father breathes in the Son and the Son in the Father, which is the Holy Spirit Himself . . . There would not be a true and total transformation if the soul were not transformed in the three Persons of the Most Holy Trinity in an open and manifest degree . . . for the soul united and transformed in God breathes out in God to God the very divine spiration which God—she being transformed in Him—breathes out in Himself to her.[8]

The prayer of unity is the deepest expression of contemplation, arising from union with God, and so it is very subtle. As described in Chapter 8, unity is, I believe, the fullness of Jesus's teaching on how to pray: the words of prayer and the movements of life emerging from the secrecy of contemplation. When you open to the attitude and experience that we live and move and have our being in God, you experience prayer and activity emerging, inseparably, together. With the receptive attitude of emerging, freedom *from* thoughts is integrated with and emerges in God along with a greater freedom *in* thoughts. This inner freedom inherently transcends the dualism of inner and outer. This same freedom arises more naturally in life. Freer from the separate-self sense, ordinary, often unseen compassion for others flows as an expression of God's nature.

Integrating and Emerging in Life

When Jim came home from the desert, his contemplative practice developed toward the intuition of unity, including more freedom in the movement of thoughts and in God's emergent action. Around this same time, Jim's job got even busier. He was under great pressure to finish the house he was building, and he couldn't find supplies or subcontractors to meet his deadline. In addition, he and his wife chose to adopt their foster child. I believe Jim's desert realization helped him to finish building his house and say yes to new responsibility in his family life. The job stress didn't necessarily disappear. The adoption process and his life as a father were not easy. But I believe that Jim's desert realization and ensuing attitudinal shift in practice helped him see and experience his ordinary life, his work, and his family duties more in God.

Six months after his desert sojourn, Jim said to me, "Dave, ordinary life is where God is. My family is where my spiritual practice is." This remains Jim's challenge and invitation for contemplative practice.

Reflective Exercise

Pause for a moment in silence and consider:

- How are you integrating prayer and activity?
- How is the divine expressing itself in your life?

Conclusion

My hope is that this book has planted some seeds that will help you on your contemplative path. If you are not a practitioner of centering prayer, I hope that this book sheds light on your own contemplative practice or the possibility of having one. Perhaps learning about the tradition of transformative practice in Christianity has inspired you. Jesus's message is not about reciting empty words of prayer from a fundamentalist perspective. Jesus's teaching includes following an inner path, in which the structures of consciousness are transformed in contemplation and through which you discover an eternal truth that has practical impact in ordinary life. From the contemplative point of view, some of the most practical benefits of the path of centering prayer are greater inner freedom, greater compassion for others, and greater humility as you accept yourself more as a human being who is in relationship with God's love and everyone else.

If you are a practitioner of centering prayer, you might find that returning to its basics with a fresh eye enriches the foundation you have already received from reading other books and attending workshops or retreats. This book may also have shown you a way of deepening your practice of centering prayer—with the sacred word, the sacred breath, or the sacred glance—and infusing it with more receptivity to the living Word, the Breath of God, the unseeable mystery of God. You may have connected with the teaching on the practice of the sacred nothingness and how it leads you into contemplation. You may have discovered that one of these ways of deepening centering prayer suits the spiritual season you are in. You may have experienced a more subtle sense of who, or what, God is. If so, I am grateful.

In order to grow and flourish, seeds need sunlight and water. The Resources section provides support for the growth of your practice. My website can point you toward other writings, Internet resources, ways of connecting with others who share your interest as a practitioner, ideas about how to pursue contemplative spiritual direction, and retreats and workshops. The Resources section also includes a link to Contemplative Outreach's website, which provides materials by Thomas Keating and others, along with a listing of introductory workshops and intensive retreats on centering prayer. If you are new to centering prayer, the appendix gives you more background on its basic guidelines through the standardized material developed by Contemplative Outreach.

Before you put this book down, I invite you to take a moment to think about how you will go forward with your practice. If you are a practitioner of centering prayer, how do you feel called to practice with the sacred symbol? At this season of your spiritual journey, are you drawn to the practice of deepening the sacred word, the sacred breath, or the sacred glance, or to practicing the sacred nothingness? Is there one of the contemplative attitudes that has particularly come alive for you? Just take a moment to review these contemplative attitudes and see if there is a word that will particularly help you as you return to your practice of centering prayer or another kind of meditation:

- God's presence consenting in you
- Simplicity
- Gentleness and effortlessness
- Letting go and letting be
- Resting and being
- Embracing and being embraced by God
- Integrating prayer

Let one of these attitudes stay with you, as a gift that you take back with you into your practice, to guide you more deeply into contemplative relationship with God.

The greatest gift on the contemplative path is God. May you realize your life in God's dance. May you embrace and be embraced by your own true partner.

Dancing in the Center of God

On my knees your love finds me
No one ever spoke such silence
Opening my hands
In despair's dusk and joy's dawning
Still you name me
Night vision transfiguring spiritual darkness
Pure gift echoing before the beginning
Love's inbreathing

In dense forest
A path reveals itself
As my true purpose
Unite us
In mind, body, heart, being
Your name, breath, image, mystery
Yes
Within yes

Turning
And returning
Simply, to only you
Through desert wildernesses, unsigned streets, broken borders
Awakening in light
Radiant, unmoving, spacious
Each step, every movement
Unturned to you

In secrecy
Gentleness is born
Without trying
Snow falls on hilltops
Without struggle
Petals open on their own
Effortlessly your body births itself in this world
Morning rain drenches blades of dew

Your name, touch, image
All, now, life for me
Yet greater mystery beckons
Letting you let go in me
The surrender of my surrender
Through obscure clouds
Into the source of your brightness
Everything ordinary is sacred

You became all
Nothing to reject as it arises in you
All I am not I become for you
Empty tomb smiles light around decay
Embracing you as a seal on my heart
Being embraced in darkness
Rainbows
Break forth from gray

You are that you are
Beyond time, just in time
Rest beyond resting
Wait beyond waiting
A flock crosses the sky
But not a single shadow falls
Be beyond being
I am that I am

Conclusion

Compassion's outbreathing
Into life, a dancing reflection
Diapers, laundry, hospice—unobtrusive prayers
This fortress yields to unseen compassion
Circle of friends now dawn in us
Secrecy shouting
Just human
As was always so

Notes

Introduction

1. Often the term "false self" is used to describe the limitations of the human condition and is contrasted with a "true self." In this book, I prefer the term "separate-self sense" because I have found that, although very descriptive, "false self" engenders in some practitioners an unhelpful attitude of resistance to their human experience. Similarly, "true self," for some practitioners, evokes goal-seeking and attachment. In trying to speak about something as ineffable as contemplation, no term is free from limitations.

Chapter 1

1. As quoted in Thomas Keating, *Open Mind, Open Heart,* 20th Anniversary edition (New York: Continuum, 2006), and in Contemplative Outreach's basic guidelines for centering prayer. All subsequent quotes from *Open Mind, Open Heart* are from this edition unless otherwise noted.
2. Laurence Freeman, *Jesus the Teacher Within* (New York: Continuum, 2000), 202.
3. John Cassian, "Conference Nine," in *Conferences: Classics of Western Spirituality,* translated by Colm Luibheid (New York: Paulist Press, 1985), 123–24.
4. Historically, the term "contemplation" or "contemplative prayer" was used in the Christian tradition to mean a way of relating with God that was not based in thoughts, concepts, or images. Traditionally, the term "meditation" was used in

Christianity to describe how to relate to God *with* thoughts, concepts, and images. Since Asian forms of contemplative practice were introduced to the West in the twentieth century, the terms "contemplation" and "meditation" are often used in Christianity in similar ways, to describe a nonconceptual way of relating to God.

5. Ken Wilber, *Integral Spirituality* (Boston: Integral Books/ Shambhala, 2006).
6. I first heard this imagery of spiritual seasons in the poetic contemplative teachings of Father Martin Laird.

Chapter 2

1. The Jerusalem Bible (Garden City, NY: Doubleday, 1966).

Chapter 3

1. Thomas Keating, *Manifesting God* (New York: Lantern Books, 2005), 109.
2. Rodger Hudleston, ed., *The Spiritual Letters of Dom John Chapman O.S.B.* (London: Sheed and Ward, 1946), 176.

Chapter 4

1. The Jerusalem Bible.
2. Keating, *Open Mind, Open Heart,* 35.
3. "The Way of Perfection," *The Collected Works of St. Teresa of Avila, Volume Two,* translated by Otilio Rodriguez and Kieran Kavanaugh (Washington, DC: ICS Publications, 1980), 156.
4. Ibid., 155.
5. Keating, *Open Mind, Open Heart,* 65.
6. Thomas Keating, *Open Mind, Open Heart* (Warwick, NY: Amity House, 1986), 74, 90–91.
7. The Jerusalem Bible.

Chapter 5

1. Keating, *Open Mind, Open Heart*, 35.
2. Ibid.
3. Dawna Markova, *The Open Mind* (Berkeley, CA: Conari Press, 1996).
4. Thomas Keating, *Invitation to Love* (Rockport, MA: Element, 1992), 66.
5. Cynthia Bourgeault, *Centering Prayer and Inner Awakening* (Cambridge, MA: Cowley Publications, 2004), 83.
6. Paul speaks about Jesus's kenosis, his self-emptying: "Though he was in the form of God, did not regard equality with God as something to be exploited, but emptied himself" (Philippians 2:6–7).
7. Bernard McGinn, *The Flowering of Mysticism* (New York: Crossroad, 1998), 207.
8. Keating, *Manifesting God*, 111–12.

Chapter 6

1. Quoted in Thomas Merton, *The Wisdom of the Desert* (New York: New Directions, 1960), 8–9.
2. Although some authors refer to God as "himself," I refer to God's self, especially in light of the Trinitarian revelation of God's personhood, by the gender-neutral "Godself."
3. Quoted in Carl Arico, *A Taste of Silence* (New York: Continuum, 1999), 35.
4. *The Collected Works of St. John of the Cross,* edited by Kieran Kavanaugh and Otilio Rodriguez (Washington, DC: ICS, 1979), 236.
5. Quoted in Paul Murray, *I Loved Jesus in the Night: Teresa of Calcutta—A Secret Revealed* (Brewster, MA: Paraclete Press, 2008), 53.

6. Adam McHugh, *Introverts in the Church* (Downers Grove, IL: Intervarsity Press, 2009).
7. Bourgeault, *Centering Prayer and Inner Awakening*, 153.
8. Keating, *Manifesting God*, 80.

Chapter 7

1. Paul points toward the completion of prayer in scripture when he writes, "Faith, hope and love last forever, but the greatest of them all is love" (1 Corinthians 13:13).
2. See Keating, *Open Mind, Open Heart*, 68–69.
3. Keating, *Manifesting God*, 111–12.
4. Louis Bouyer cites one early writer, Clement of Alexandria, in this regard: "The Word of God was made man so that we might learn how men may become God." *The Christian Mystery* (Petersham, MA: St. Bede's Publications, 1990), 147.
5. Keating, *Manifesting God*, 112.
6. *The Collected Works of St. John of the Cross*, 120.
7. Thomas Merton, *New Seeds of Contemplation* (Boston: Shambhala, 2003), 289–90.

Chapter 8

1. New American Standard Bible (La Habra, CA: Lockman Foundation, 1995).

Chapter 9

1. Merton, *New Seeds of Contemplation*, 41.
2. Thomas Merton, letter to Abdul Aziz, 2 January 1966, in *The Hidden Ground of Love: The Letters of Thomas Merton on Religious Experience and Social Concerns*, edited by William H. Shannon (New York: Farrar, Straus & Giroux, 1985), 62–64.
3. Keating, *Open Mind, Open Heart*, 7.
4. Merton, *New Seeds of Contemplation*, 41.

5. Thomas Merton, *A Search for Solitude: Pursuing the Monk's True Life; The Journals of Thomas Merton, Volume 3, 1952–1960* (San Francisco: HarperSanFrancisco, 1997), 181–83.

Chapter 10

1. Keating, *Manifesting God,* 3.
2. T. S. Eliot, *Four Quartets* (Orlando, FL: Harcourt, 1943).

Chapter 11

1. *The Cloud of Unknowing,* translated by Clifton Wolters (Baltimore: Penguin, 1961), 60.
2. Ibid., 61–62.
3. Meister Eckhart, *Selected Writings,* translated by Oliver Davies (New York: Penguin, 1994).
4. *The Cloud of Unknowing,* 59.
5. Ibid., 58.
6. Andrew Harvey, ed., *Teachings of the Christian Mystics* (Boston: Shambhala, 1998), 126.

Chapter 12

1. John Ruusbroec, in Harvey, ed., *Teachings of the Christian Mystics,* 117.
2. St. Francis de Sales, cited in *Francis de Sales, Jane de Chantal: Letters of Spiritual Direction* (New York: Paulist Press, 1998), 64.

Chapter 13

1. Gerald May, *Addiction and Grace* (New York: HarperOne, 1988), 17.
2. Keating, *Open Mind, Open Heart,* 39, 41.

Chapter 14

1. David Steindl-Rast, "Man of Prayer," in *Thomas Merton, Monk: Monastic Tribute,* edited by Patrick Hart (New York: Sheed and Ward, 1974), 83–84.

2. Thomas Merton, "As Man to Man," *Cistercian Studies* 4, no. 1 (1969), 93–94. Also quoted in James Finley, *Merton's Palace of Nowhere* (Notre Dame, IN: Ave Maria Press, 1978), 109.

Chapter 15

1. Some of the somatically based psychotherapies for releasing trauma now being practiced and researched include sensorimotor psychotherapy, somatic experiencing, and eye movement desensitization and reprocessing (EMDR).
2. Keating, *Open Mind, Open Heart,* 101.
3. Gregory the Great, commentary on Job 4:13, in Bernard McGinn, ed., *The Essential Writings of Christian Mysticism* (New York: Random House, 2006), 369–70.
4. If you experience strong trauma in centering prayer, it can be valuable to seek support in psychotherapy from someone trained in dealing with trauma who also supports your contemplative path, or from a contemplative spiritual director who understands the effects of trauma.
5. Thomas Keating, *Reawakenings* (New York: Crossroad, 1992), 103.
6. Bernadette Roberts, *What Is Self? A Study of the Spiritual Journey in Terms of Consciousness* (Boulder, CO: Sentinent, 2005), 177.

Chapter 16

1. Keating, *Open Mind, Open Heart,* 178.
2. Harvey, ed., *Teachings of the Christian Mystics,* 126.
3. Keating, *Manifesting God,* x.
4. See, for example, Ilia Delio, *Christ in Evolution* (New York: Orbis, 2008).
5. Harvey, ed., *Teachings of the Christian Mystics,* 67.
6. Laurence Freeman, *First Sight: The Experience of Faith* (New York: Continuum, 2011), 120.

7. Harvey, ed., *Teachings of the Christian Mystics*, 118.
8. John of the Cross, *The Spiritual Canticle*, stanza 39:3, 4. In *The Collected Works of St. John of the Cross*, 558.

APPENDIX: THE BASIC GUIDELINES OF CENTERING PRAYER

The following information is excerpted from an informational pamphlet on centering prayer titled "The Method of Centering Prayer: The Prayer of Consent," by Thomas Keating. The full pamphlet be found on the website for Contemplative Outreach, contemplativeoutreach.org.

Be still and know that I am God.

—Psalm 46:10

Contemplative Prayer

We may think of prayer as thoughts or feelings expressed in words. But this is only one expression. In the Christian tradition Contemplative Prayer is considered to be the pure gift of God. It is the opening of mind and heart—our whole being—to God, the Ultimate Mystery, beyond thoughts, words, and emotions. Through grace we open our awareness to God whom we know by faith is within us, closer than breathing, closer than thinking, closer than choosing—closer than consciousness itself.

Centering Prayer

Centering Prayer is a method designed to facilitate the development of Contemplative Prayer by preparing our faculties to receive this gift. It is an attempt to present the teaching of earlier times in an updated form. Centering Prayer is not meant to replace other kinds of prayer; rather it casts a new light and depth of meaning on them. It is at the same time a relationship with God and a discipline to foster that relationship. This method of prayer is a movement beyond conversation with Christ to communion with Him.

Theological Background

The source of Centering Prayer, as in all methods leading to Contemplative Prayer, is the indwelling Trinity: Father, Son, and Holy Spirit. The focus of Centering Prayer is the deepening of our relationship with the living Christ. It tends to build communities of faith and bond the members together in mutual friendship and love.

The Root of Centering Prayer

Listening to the word of God in Scripture (Lectio Divina) is a traditional way of cultivating friendship with Christ. It is a way of listening to the texts of Scripture as if we were in conversation with Christ and He were suggesting the topics of conversation. The daily encounter with Christ and reflection on His word leads beyond mere acquaintanceship to an attitude of friendship, trust, and love. Conversation simplifies and gives way to communing. Gregory the Great (6th century) in summarizing the Christian contemplative tradition expressed it as "resting in God." This was the classical meaning of Contemplative Prayer in the Christian tradition for the first sixteen centuries.

Wisdom Saying of Jesus

Centering Prayer is based on the wisdom saying of Jesus in the Sermon on the Mount:

". . . But when you pray, go to your inner room, close the door and pray to your Father in secret. And your Father, who sees in secret, will reward you" (Matthew 6:6).

It is also inspired by writings of major contributors to the Christian contemplative heritage, including John Cassian, the anonymous author of *The Cloud of Unknowing*, Francis de Sales, Teresa of Avila, John of the Cross, Thérèse of Lisieux, and Thomas Merton.

The Guidelines

1. Choose a sacred word as the symbol of your intention to consent to God's presence and action within.

2. Sitting comfortably and with eyes closed, settle briefly and silently introduce the sacred word as the symbol of your consent to God's presence and action within.

3. When engaged with your thoughts (which include body sensations, feelings, images, and reflections), return ever so gently to the sacred word.

4. At the end of the prayer period, remain in silence with eyes closed for a couple of minutes.

Centering Prayer Guidelines

I. Choose a sacred word as the symbol of your intention to consent to God's presence and action within. *(Open Mind, Open Heart,* Thomas Keating)

1. The sacred word expresses our intention to consent to God's presence and action within.

2. The sacred word is chosen during a brief period of prayer to the Holy Spirit. Use a word of one or two syllables, such as: God, Jesus, Abba, Father, Mother, Mary, Amen. Other possibilities include: Love, Listen, Peace, Mercy, Let Go, Silence, Stillness, Faith, Trust.

3. Instead of a sacred word, a simple inward glance toward the Divine Presence, or noticing one's breath may be more suitable for some persons. The same guidelines apply to these symbols as to the sacred word.

4. The sacred word is sacred not because of its inherent meaning, but because of the meaning we give it as the expression of our intention to consent.

5. Having chosen a sacred word, we do not change it during the prayer period because that would be engaging thoughts.

II. Sitting comfortably and with eyes closed, settle briefly and silently introduce the sacred word as the symbol of your consent to God's presence and action within.

1. "Sitting comfortably" means relatively comfortably so as not to encourage sleep during the time of prayer.

2. Whatever sitting position we choose, we keep the back straight.

3. We close our eyes as a symbol of letting go of what is going on around and within us.

4. We introduce the sacred word inwardly as gently as laying a feather on a piece of absorbent cotton.

5. Should we fall asleep, upon awakening we continue the prayer.

III. When engaged with your thoughts, return ever so gently to the sacred word.

1. "Thoughts" is an umbrella term for every perception, including body sensations, sense perceptions, feelings, images, memories, plans, reflections, concepts, commentaries, and spiritual experiences.

2. Thoughts are an inevitable, integral, and normal part of Centering Prayer.

3. By "returning ever so gently to the sacred word" a minimum of effort is indicated. This is the only activity we initiate during the time of Centering Prayer.

4. During the course of Centering Prayer, the sacred word may become vague or disappear.

IV. At the end of the prayer period, remain in silence with eyes closed for a couple of minutes.

1. The additional two minutes enables us to bring the atmosphere of silence into everyday life.

2. If this prayer is done in a group, the leader may slowly recite a prayer such as the Lord's Prayer, while the others listen.

Resources for Beginning or Continuing Your Centering Prayer Practice

David Frenette's website, which you can access via incarnational-contemplation.com or davidfrenette.com, provides information to help you continue with the teachings introduced in this book and other materials on contemplative practice, including:

- Other writing by David Frenette

- Internet resources

- Ways of connecting with others who share your interest as a practitioner

- How to receive personal guidance in these teachings from David Frenette and others trained in their practice

- Retreats and workshops on deepening centering prayer

- Material on other contemplative practices that complements the practice of deepening centering prayer and helps you realize unity in God

- Additional resources as they are developed

The Incarnational Contemplation Project and David Frenette continue to research and develop resources and practices for the contemplative path. If you would like to support this work, please visit the donation page of the websites. Thank you.

For information and resources on Father Thomas Keating and getting started in centering prayer, contact:

Contemplative Outreach, Ltd.
10 Park Place, 2nd Floor, Suite B
Butler, NJ 07405
Telephone: (973) 838-3384
Fax: (973) 492-5795
Email: office@coutreach.org

Visit contemplativeoutreach.org for event and retreat listings, articles, and the online bookstore.

About the Author

David Frenette is a meditation counselor, writer, and guide whose works include a companion audio series to this book, *Centering Prayer Meditations*, published by Sounds True.

David began searching for meaning as a young man in the 1970s when he started practicing daily meditation in Hindu and Buddhist traditions. He had a series of awakening experiences to Christ, changed his contemplative practice to centering prayer, and became a Christian in 1981. In 1983, he met Father Thomas Keating, the Trappist monk, teacher, and founder of centering prayer, who became his mentor and whom he still considers to be his spiritual father, or *abba*.

David co-created and co-led a contemplative retreat center for ten years under Father Keating's auspices. He taught centering prayer there and at retreat centers around the country for thirty years. He has served in many leadership and consultative roles within Contemplative Outreach, Father Keating's international organization, including guiding long-term centering prayer practitioners. He taught in the Religious Studies Department at Naropa University for six years and was involved with the Integral Institute as a founding member.

Although David still dedicates significant time each day to solitary meditation, after spending many years in monastic retreat, he increasingly experiences the sacred in the ordinariness of everyday life. He enjoys friendship, music, film, ocean walks, coffee shops, and life in the Pacific Northwest with his wife, Donna.

Trained as a transpersonal counseling psychologist, the focus of his work now is on integrating the path of meditation with psychology and life-in-the-world. David offers spiritual direction to clients worldwide and is currently developing online resources for Christian meditators and other spiritual seekers. One of David's current interests is extracting the essence of the Christian mystical/contemplative tradition, making its practices more accessible to contemporary seekers who are "spiritual, not religious."

For more information on David's work, visit his website: davidfrenette.com.

About Sounds True

Sounds True is a multimedia publisher whose mission is to inspire and support personal transformation and spiritual awakening. Founded in 1985 and located in Boulder, Colorado, we work with many of the leading spiritual teachers, thinkers, healers, and visionary artists of our time. We strive with every title to preserve the essential "living wisdom" of the author or artist. It is our goal to create products that not only provide information to a reader or listener, but that also embody the quality of a wisdom transmission.

For those seeking genuine transformation, Sounds True is your trusted partner. At SoundsTrue.com you will find a wealth of free resources to support your journey, including exclusive weekly audio interviews, free downloads, interactive learning tools, and other special savings on all our titles.

To learn more, please visit SoundsTrue.com/freegifts or call us toll-free at 800.333.9185.